A54 - 2

SO-FIW-431

BÉLA BARTÓK

Végh Sándornak.
emlékül
Budapest, 1940 okt 10
Bartók Béla

BÉLA BARTÓK

by

SERGE MOREUX

Preface by

ARTHUR HONEGGER

NAZARETH COLLEGE
LIBRARY
WITHDRAWN

HARVILL PRESS · LONDON

Translated from the French by

G. S. FRASER *and* ERIK DE MAUNY

35648

ALL RIGHTS RESERVED

Published by
The Harvill Press
23 Lower Belgrave Street
London, S.W.1
1953

Printed in Great Britain by
The Alcuin Press, Welwyn Garden City, Herts

n86.4
Bar
mor

CONTENTS

Lond, Harvill ~ $1.20 (ste.)

ILLUSTRATIONS

PREFACE

I FIRST met Béla Bartók in 1911 at Zürich when I was studying at the Conservatoire there. During a *Tonkünstlerfest* concert a slimly-built man, with delicate features and clear eyes, took a seat beside me while the orchestra was playing, and then, when the piece was finished, went up on the stage and played his *Rhapsody for Pianoforte and Orchestra* under the baton of Volkmar Andrae. At once I was captivated: how fresh the colour and rhythmic the life of this work, so unlike the many similarly entitled pieces which then encumbered the repertoires.

Soon I had the opportunity of studying the piano *Bagatelles* (Op. 6), and I must confess that I was somewhat disconcerted by the surprising liberty of their idiom. Since then I have been able to familiarize myself with the work of this great Hungarian musician, and, from the *Second Quartet* to the *Music for Strings and Percussion*, my admiration has steadily grown. Soon after its publication, the quartet was performed by Yvonne Giraud, Delgrange, Darius Milhaud and myself, not without faults, for the work is quite difficult. Highly interesting, we found it, indeed we of the younger musical generation were captivated by Bartók, and to listen to a fresh work of his became an event, alas too rare, of capital importance.

Most writers have agreed to hold Schönberg and Stravinsky responsible for the reaction which set in after Debussy. Some have included Erik Satie; I personally would nominate Bartók instead. These three are the authentic representatives of the musical revolution of that generation. Less direct and sparkling than Stravinsky, less dogmatic than Schönberg, Bartók is perhaps the most profoundly musical of the three and best manifests a close-knit organic development.

He had a decided bent towards works of what are called pure music; one result is that his importance to us is as enduring as that of Schönberg and Stravinsky, though its impact is less brusque. Not that his music can be grasped at first attempt, for not all performers are capable of rendering it; and its extraordinary rhythmic subtlety calls for a greater effort at precision than does classical music; the alternation of very diverse metres in rapid succession demands sustained attention from player and listener, both of whom may be baffled by their variety. The attempt to do justice to them may incur the reproach of lacking rhythm and sacrificing everything in an attempt to produce an effect of excitement. The charge, however, cannot be levelled at the works themselves, for their internal poise is secure and quite convincing. Nor need we ever be haunted by the suspicion that the composer is out to isolate from his experience a merely technical exercise, for his temper is rich and warm, and the clouds are shot through with high and moving beams.

The development proceeds in a synthesis of different elements, harmonic, rhythmic, melodic, all of which are brought out in turn; one may predominate for some passages but without swamping another, which presently comes out in its proper place. But irregularity is much less frequent than might be expected, and M. Moreux rightly emphasizes the point, which bears on Bartók's characteristic genius, not his shortcomings. He is not sufficiently known or rightly appreciated, and this penetrating study of his work will be welcome. I hope it will help to bring his name into concert programmes more frequently, for close and warm literary exposition of music is never a substitute for actual listening to its sounds. May this book have the effect of giving the musical public more and more opportunities of admiring and coming to love the magic of Béla Bartók.

ARTHUR HONEGGER

CHAPTER ONE

EARLY YEARS

CHILDHOOD AND YOUTH, 1881–99

BÉLA BARTÔK was born on the 25th March, 1881, at Nagyszenmiklos,[1] in the region of Torontál, a part of Hungary annexed by Rumania at the Treaty of Trianon, a plainland of rich cornfields and pastures stretching to the Danube from the last folds of the Carpathian foothills. His father was the head of the agricultural school there, a man of pronounced musical tastes, who played the piano agreeably and learned the 'cello in order to take his part in the amateur orchestra he had founded; he also tried his hand at composing dance music. He died when Béla was nine years old. His widow, Paula Bartók (*née* Voit) was compelled to earn a living for herself and her two children, Béla and Elizabeth. She secured a post as schoolmistress at Nagyszöllös, now in Czechoslovakia, a poorly paid position which entailed a struggle for the mother of a family.

Little is known for certain about Béla's childhood. He was set to learn the piano when six years old. He is reticent about himself in his short *Curriculum Vitae* and *Autobiography*.[2]

---

[1] Often referred to in Bartók's writings as Sânnicolaul Mare.
[2] The *Curriculum Vitae Succinct* stops at December, 1905, when

His fame at his death prompted a host of memoirs, of which the most recent is of great importance, namely an article by Károly Kristóf entitled *Scherzo, Spring Song, Valse: unknown works by Bartók brought to light.*[1] Before briefly describing these works, the author repeats the reminiscences of Endre Nagy's young sister. Endre Nagy was Bartók's childhood friend, and the accuracy of his sister's recollections is confirmed by their allusions to lost compositions which have since been discovered.

She describes how the inhabitants of Nagyszöllös learned to like the friendly schoolmistress, who did the cooking, washing and mending for her household, and who would sit up late over her worktable in order to make the children's clothes. Hungary was an integral part of the Hapsburg Empire, but the spirit of separatism seized every opportunity of expression. Until 1891 no public celebration was permitted of the 15th March—the

---

it was written at the instance of a journalist, Géza Meyer. It was not published until the 7th March, 1922 in the daily newspaper *Sopronvarmegye.* The original is preserved in the town museum of Sopron. The first version of the *Autobiography* first appeared in German in the *Musikpädagogische Zeitschrift* (1918), the definitive text, also in German, in the number of the *Musikblätter des Anbruchs* (Vienna, 1st March, 1922), devoted to Bartók, and then in the slim volume, *Autobiography, Musical Writings,* published by the University Press of Budapest in 1946.

Despite their ambiguities and gaps these writings are important for they give Bartók's own account of his development.

[1] *Magyar Nemzet*—"The Hungarian Nation"—29th June 1952.

anniversary of the 1848 Revolution—and even then it was confined to the classroom, and the day was not a school holiday. The schoolmaster, Gábor Nagy, set himself to draw up a programme, and Béla Bartók, then ten years old, was brought in. Unexpectedly the school inspector decided that the feast should be postponed, and accordingly it took place in the middle of the night. It began with the National Song of Alexander Petofi,[1] and then the boy sat at the piano to play a valse of his own composition, which in fact was the first declaration of his musical power. Prolonged applause greeted him; and his encores included works by himself and others. Finally the schoolmaster announced that the little boy was too tired to go on.

The reminiscences go on to tell how Madame Bartók came one day to Madame Nagy and asked that Endre should do some looking after Béla during the summer holidays. Both boys were at college together at Nagyvárad, and were about to come home together at the end of the term. When they arrived, Endre could not stop talking about Béla, who was four years younger than himself. The two boys would go for walks together; the elder, who was thinking of becoming a painter, would take palette, canvas and easel, and as he worked the younger would lie on the grass and listen to the song of the birds.

In his *Autobiography* Bartók records that he

---

[1] 1823–49. The most famous national poet of the period.

composed small pieces from the age of nine, and that he himself performed some at the Nagyszöllös concert. The *Curriculum Vitae* mentions that he took lessons from Kersch while a boarder at Nagyvárad with the encouragement of Altdörfer who had discovered his talent. Until the appearance of Kristóf's article and the first volume of Bartók's correspondence with his mother, edited by Demény, it was generally assumed that Zoltán Kodály was primarily responsible for the beginnings of the revival of folk-music. Insufficient regard was paid to the statement in the *Autobiography*, "In 1905 I began to explore the peasant music of Hungary, which until then might be called unknown. Here I had the good fortune to find a first-rate collaborator in Zoltán Kodály." The rest of Kristóf's article, confirmed by a letter of 1st April, 1903, asking for information about a popular melody, leads us to the definite conclusion that Bartók, whether closely or not, was always occupied with folk-music.

Endre Nagy, according to his sister, was employed as a harvest overseer for the fields about Nagyszöllös on the banks of the Tisza which belonged to the Abony-Lator family. The seasonal workers came from the Verkhovine (middle territory). Every year their leader presented himself before the bailiff to settle the terms of work for his people who presently arrived, men and women, in time for the harvest. The women wore ample white linen smocks caught in at the waist with a brightly coloured cotton belt, and the men wore white shirts tucked into wide leather belts holding pipe, tobacco, knife and comb. All lived together in a large barn; in the evening they would sit in a circle round a large cauldron of vegetable soup, and endlessly sing a song of mixed Hungarian and Slav words.

> *Maramaros dobri varos i dobre iam zsiti,*
> *Jeszt palinku i jeszt chleba,*
> *Ne treba platiti.*
> *Tiitii titiii. . . .*

This song they would sing also while they worked. One day, when Nagy took Béla to the fields, the boy wrote down in pencil the musical score, and urged the workers to sing other songs. But always they came back to this their only one, not that it was entirely native, since it was mixed with Hungarian words.

In 1892 Madame Bartók became schoolmistress at Beszterce, in what is now Rumanian Transylvania, and in 1893 she was appointed to a department of the High School of Pozsony, now Bratislava in Czechoslovakia; this marked an important step in Bartók's life. "In those days," he writes in his *Autobiography*, "among all the Hungarian provincial towns Pozsony enjoyed the most flourishing musical life. László Erkel, the third son of Ferenc Erkel,[1]

---

[1] 1810–93. After the appearance of his opera, *Bánk bán*, which contains elements of folk-music, he enjoyed the highest reputation among Hungarian musicians. He became Director of the Budapest Conservatoire.

B

taught me harmony and the piano until my
fifteenth year, and saw to it that I went to operas
and symphony concerts; these were of varying
quality. Nor did I neglect to take part in chamber
music, so that by my eighteenth year I was pretty
well acquainted with music scores from Bach to
Wagner but only so far as *Tannhäuser*. Between
whiles I applied myself to composition; I was
strongly influenced by Brahms and by Dohnányi,
who was four years older than me, and whose first
work made a deep impression on me."[1]

Two less famous composers, Burger and Hyrtl,
may also be mentioned in passing; they were not
without influence on the young Bartók's musical
formation. Little, however, is known about his
early essays; his allusions to them are slighting.
Indeed throughout his correspondence one is
struck by the absence of musical self-analysis; circumstances of composition may be hinted at, and
reflections about musical form in general may be
offered, but these grow scantier as he grows older.
On this account, what Kristóf has to say of his
early works is of special interest. All were dedicated
to Gabrielle de Lator, doubtless a daughter of the
landowning family over whose fields he strolled
with his friend Endre Nagy during the summer
holidays at Nagyszöllös.

The first of the four works, and the best, is the

---

[1] Ernst Dohnányi, born at Pozsony in 1877, who has been
called "the Hungarian Brahms", despite his impressionist and
folklore style.

Scherzo, a piano duet in D minor, which lasts about three minutes.[1] The melody recalls Schumann. It gives promise of his energy, but not of his later style. The other compositions are transcribed in his mother's hand. One is a little piece, *Spring Song*, in six-eight time, another is entitled *Walzer*, in German, the last *Drei Klavierstücke von Bartók, Béla*, 1897, of which the first movement is marked *presto*, the third *adagio*, while no indication of tempo is given to the second. There is talk of publishing them; their interest is considerable, for they would help us to observe the progress of straining and purifying in the musical development of a master.

It is believed that he destroyed all his youthful compositions. Nevertheless some copies survived, including those received by the persons to whom they were dedicated. An early piano sonata, dated 1898, and influenced by Brahms has been reported, and Bartók refers in a letter of August, 1898, to three melodies for voice accompanied by piano. A pupil of his has told me that the words were from poems by Heine.

"After having finished with school," says the *Autobiography*, "I was faced with a choice. At which Conservatoire should I continue my musical education? At Pozsony in those days the Vienna Conservatoire was regarded as the only one main musical stronghold. Nevertheless I followed Dohnányi' advice, and chose Budapest." He was to congratu-

---

[1] *Scherzo für das Pianoforte componiert und dem Fraülein Gabrielle v. Lator gewidmet von Béla Bartók*, Comp. 1897.

late himself on this decision. "I would not give anything for the entire Vienna Conservatoire. One day when I was telling Professor Thomán about Dohnányi's advice, and how well content I was not to have gone to Vienna, he capped me with the story of a highly gifted girl who had finished her studies at the Vienna Conservatoire and been given a distinction at her examination, but when she came to Budapest, as he witnessed for himself, she knew nothing and regretted she had not come to Budapest sooner." It was in the Autumn of 1899 that Bartók entered the Budapest Conservatoire, then styled the Academy Liszt.

AT THE BUDAPEST CONSERVATOIRE, 1899–1903

His technical training for the piano was completed under István Thomán, a pupil of Liszt. He attended the classes on composition given by Janos Koessler, a cousin of Max Reger, Paul Hindemith's first master and a post-romantic German composer devoted to Bach. Bartók much admired Koessler, gave him his entire confidence, and submitted to him his compositions for consideration, advice and discussion.

"Yesterday," he wrote to his mother, 5th January, 1900, "I took the quintet to Koessler who decided that the ensemble was not good and told me not to go on with it, but turn instead to simpler tasks such as melodies. Not good—that I pass over, for he did not descend from generalities, but merely remarked that I should make a better choice of themes, and so forth. If it be true that the work contains no theme of any significance, I fail to see how in a year's time I shall be capable of writing anything of importance. Why did he not tell me last January that these pieces were of no value? My opinion is that the quintet is at all points better than last year's quartet. I myself think that my compositions are good substantially, and that correction is required only on details of form. It is really too bad if they are too poor to stand correction."

This letter, which serves to date two compositions hitherto unpublished, shows how seriously he was working. Apart from his hard practising to be a virtuoso, he was under the necessity of giving piano lessons. He went through the drudgery of a student with limited resources. The work was ill-paid. "The young lady has stopped her lessons for the present," he wrote to his mother, 16th January, 1900, "because her piano needs tuning. After that she wants to go on—if it really comes to anything. In that case, I shall ask one and a half florins and give only two lessons. If that does not suit, then she can do what she likes. The bore is that she has not paid what is owing. Friday last I found I was without funds, and decided I would not wait, but demand, so on the Saturday I tried to get the money, so far no success. Here in my lodgings I drum my fingers; how monstrous of her not to send the money when I am without it. If

two florins come to-day, perhaps the rest will
follow in three days."

Fortune smiled later when he became the teacher
of Madame Gruber, a good pianist and a woman
of taste possessing good contacts in the musical
world; she was the future wife of Zoltán Kodály,
Bartók's friend and counsellor. But his toil spelled
the sacrifice of pleasures; the following letter to
his mother, 17th January, 1903, reveals his tired-
ness and also his lively sarcastic humour. "Now a
story for Aunt Irma.[1] Dohnányi has recommended
a remedy against fatigue, Elliman's Embrocation,
equally good for all kinds of muscular pain and
rheumatism, for a stiff neck and so forth. You can
buy it at any chemist for 90 kreutzers. Directions
for use are given in English and Hungarian. It
begins, 'Manner of employing Royal Elliman's
Embrocation for cows, sheep, horses, donkeys, and
birds'. This makes me muse, where do musicians
come in? To-morrow I lunch with the Gárdonyis,
and in the afternoon I go on to the Arányis, but I
shall not stay long for I have much to do. Anyhow
it is carnival time, and it is dangerous to dally with
girls for they easily lead one a dance."

The famous were not spared his teasing spirit.
Take, for instance, his observations on Sauer, the
celebrated pianist and a social lion, sent to his
mother, 21st January, 1900. "I have heard Sauer
and seen him. But I am at a loss to decide, who
plays better, he or d'Albert, for what I like most

---

[1] His mother's sister.

with d'Albert, namely Bach and Beethoven, was
not in the programme. What Sauer played, he
played in truly magnificent style. That one piano
could produce such unusual sonorities scarcely
seemed possible. Schumann, Chopin, Liszt—all
very beautiful, all carried me away, whereas when
d'Albert played the Bohemian Airs of Tausig he
pleased me least. Above all, Sauer enraptured the
ladies, all of whom agreed that he played a hundred
times better than d'Albert. Professor Thomán also
was pleased, but grudgingly, for he is no friend of
Sauer. At the end of the concert the audience
wanted Sauer at all costs to play the *Tannhäuser*
overture, but he was whacked out and would not.
What is striking is his comportment. He lifts his
hands a yard in the air, wags his head from side to
side, ponders over each piece; then, as if suddenly
realizing he must play something, he attacks it.
At the end, he raises his hands high up and then
lets them fall on his knees—perhaps these manner-
isms are what attract the ladies."

Bartók went out often, to concerts, operas,
receptions. It was all new, but necessary to the
country boy; yet, as he confessed to his mother,
16th January, 1900, "it all whacks your absent
one". The *Autobiography* tells how, from the start,
he sets himself zealously to discover Wagner—the
Ring, *Tristan*, the *Meistersinger*—as well as the
orchestral compositions of Liszt. The first Budapest
performance of *Tristan*, which took place soon after
his entry into the Conservatoire, made an enormous

impression on him: years afterwards he told me that himself, and added, "and now you French, who are beginning to free yourselves from the Wagnerian yoke, will appreciate how far we were from modern music".

All the same, Wagner's influence was merely technical; in a letter to his mother, 18th February, 1900, Bartók indicated what attracted him. "Last Monday I listened carefully to a rendering of the *Rheingold* at the Conservatoire. It is a legacy from Liszt, very interesting, full of instructive lessons, all new to me. A vast number of instruments. A beautiful ensemble! Some passages have more than thirty lines of score. Whether that is significant I do not know—people now say that it is of no great consequence. Professor Szabó always needs music paper scored with sixty lines, for he uses that number of instruments."

The *Autobiography* acknowledges that he was doing little creative work during this period. "Freed from the style of Brahms, I was unable to find the fresh path I wanted to climb through Wagner and Liszt. Not yet had I grasped Liszt's true importance for the further development of music; I appreciated only his outward show. So, for about two years, I composed nothing, and was known at the Conservatoire just as a brilliant pianist." He appeared as a soloist at a Conservatoire Concert, 18th December, 1902, when he played the great Sonata of Schumann.

"What roused me from torpor, like a clap of

thunder, was the first performance at Budapest in 1902 of *So Sprach Zarathustra*. The work, received with horror by most people who heard it, wrought me to a pitch of enthusiasm. I felt a reaching out to something new. I threw myself into the study of Strauss." Such was the origin of his second aesthetic orientation, first Brahms, now Strauss. Against the advice of his teachers he settled his programmes as a virtuoso accordingly. Piano transcriptions were a fashion and, as Liszt had set himself to reveal Wagner on the piano, so Bartók did the same for his favourite master, and brought Strauss to the attention and approbation of the musical public.

He wrote to his mother, 17th January, 1903, about his forthcoming appearance before one of the most considerable musical associations in Europe—his first important concert, at the Vienna Tonkünstlerverein, on 26th January. "After class, we were taken by Koessler into the large auditorium and there I played *Ein Heldenleben*. He said he was amazed that I should know all that machinery by heart and discoursed against *Ein Heldenleben*. All the same he was not unfriendly, anyway he did not seek to convince me, only to express his own opinion. Quite so; everybody has a right to that. To-day I met the 'great critic', Aurél Kern, in the tram. I was carrying the score of *Ein Heldenleben*, and seeing it he exclaimed, 'They tell me you played it like a young god'. I also talked to him about my coming visit to Vienna."

During this period he was occupied in assimilating

Strauss, and there is little evidence that he was composing; though the *Autobiography* refers vaguely to a now unknown Sonata for Violin and Piano.

Another factor which exercised a decisive influence on his musical development is indicated in the *Autobiography*. "The stream of Hungarian nationalism was then rising, and spreading into the regions of art. It reached me, and swept me into the study of our folk-music, or, more accurately, to what was then considered to be our folk-music." It was at this time that he began to consider using popular music. His taste was undistracted by the exotic, as appears in his remarks on Dohnányi's First Symphony. He writes to his mother, 9th January, 1903: "It sounds magnificent. He conducted it in excellent style, and it was much applauded. Friday's *Esti Ujsàg* published an editorial, inspired by Aurél Kern, entitled 'Ernást Dohnányi', but the good fellow makes a mistake in attributing the creation of classical Hungarian music to him, for it already existed and in a hundred places. Only his second movement is truly Hungarian; you might say the same of the first, but not of the last three."

Here he touches on the problem of authentically national music. Many obstacles and struggles had to be faced, and new openings made before the solution was found, in Hungary as elsewhere. Nobody was then prepared to welcome it; even the terms of the problem were not properly defined. For unlike literature and poetry, which for fifty

years had been going back to their sources, Hungarian music had not yet found itself by drawing on its
best elements. Some musicians, for instance the
Erkels, father and son, occasionally borrowed from
folk-songs, but the national idiom was drowned in
a flood of sonatas, symphonies, concertos, rhapsodies, operas and musical comedies, in the German,
Italian and Gypsy tradition; for, despite the belief
of the generation after Liszt, tzigane music has
really nothing in common with Hungarian folk-
music.

At that time excellent German masters were
teaching in Budapest; many of the Hungarians
themselves had learned their craft at Munich,
Dresden, Leipzig and Vienna. They liked their
music thematic, well thought out, properly composed and academic; they considered that the
songs from the plain of the *puszta* and the mountains
of the Carpathians were but decorative pieces
all'ungarese, nursery stuff, which they confused with
gypsy romance and accordingly rejected as outmoded exoticism. This misunderstanding was not
peculiar to Hungary. A century and a half of
German genius and half a century of widespread
romanticism lay heavily: so far as central Europe
is concerned the thread of Ariadne running through
the neo-Wagnerian labyrinth is found only in
Dvorák and Smetana.

From 1903 onwards the student can perceive in
Bartók's compositions that received academic ideas
were beginning to break up and the influence of

Strauss to weaken. He wrote to his mother, 4th March, 1903: "Last week a young man congratulated me, telling me that he was recently with a musical group in Vienna in company with Hanslick. The conversation turned on me and *Ein Heldenleben;* Hanslick let fall the observation that I was certainly an agreeable musician, but what a pity it was that I wasted myself over Strauss. At half-past four last Saturday afternoon I went to give Madame Gruber her lesson, and found her with Dohnányi. Before I had arrived she had played for him my piece for piano. When he came in she was in the middle of playing an interesting passage, at once he said, 'What is that? What are you playing that I have never heard before?' He went across to the piano to see, but Madame Gruber had time to conceal it among other sheets of music. Then afterwards, she played it through entirely, while Dohnányi walked up and down, asking himself whose work it could be. Suddenly he exclaimed, 'I've got it! The work is either Strauss's or Bartók's!' So then, he had found it like Strauss, and declared that it was beautiful but bizarre. Madame Gruber has always liked it, and so now does Thomán, who says that it recalls Brahms. Dohnányi now says that it is like Tchaikovsky modernized. Professor Herzfeld, to whom Madame Gruber played it on another occasion, says it is like Liszt. Somebody else thought it Wagnerian. In short, none of them had anything to go on, for the fact of the matter is that it is not

at all a pastiche though it contains some oddities."
The piece in question without doubt was one of
the Burlesques for Piano which has since been
lost.

The then reigning authorities were struck by the
young musician's personality.   Godowsky, for
instance, a pianist adored by two continents, after
having heard a movement from the Sonata for
left hand alone, exclaimed that it sounded as if it
were played with three hands, and prophesied
great things of Bartók.   Koessler, also, had a high
opinion of it; Bartók wrote to his mother, 15th
February, 1903, "he was satisfied, said it was my
best work—?!—up to the present, and that he had
nothing to correct, either in manner or matter."

He can be believed when he reports a compli-
mentary opinion for if anything his tendency was
to water it down.   He was modest and would also
pass on hostile criticisms.   Writing from Budapest
to his mother, 1st April, 1903, he said, "The
flattering words about me in the *Tagblatt* are not
worth congratulating me about.   They were written
by one of my classmates last year.   His knowledge
of music is moderate.   I enclose the programme.   A
memorable date; the first time I was presented in
public as a composer.   The *Pesti Napló* went for my
work, saying it was full of yawning gaps; on the
other hand it praised my playing.   Two *encores*
were forced on me; the second I played by heart,
for I was not prepared.   I chose one of Chopin's
Etudes, which I had not played for three months.

But it went well enough. If only they knew what
I am engaged in writing in Viennese mode, then
perhaps even the Aurél Kerns would have more
to say against me!" (This is probably an allusion
to his Kossuth Symphony, and perhaps to the
passage it contains which caricatures the Imperial
Austrian Hymn.)

Mention is made during his correspondence of
1903 of the Burlesques for Piano, which have not
been recovered yet, and of the *Sonata for Violin
and Piano*, which was first given in public at
Budapest, 26th April, 1903, with Professor Herzfeld
taking the violin part, Bartók at the piano. He
wrote to his mother on the same day. "I told you
on my Saturday's picture-postcard that your good
wishes had reached me. I also told you that my
Sonata for Violin was to be played to-day. It is
over. Unfortunately Dohnányi, Lichtenberg and
others were there. I did not allow for that, knowing
how difficult was the violin part and indeed the
general ensemble and that the first performance
could not be good, as in the event it was not.
Professor Herzfeld made many mistakes. All the
same it almost came off."

A third important work of the year appeared in
the autumn. It was a Scherzo orchestrated at
Koessler's request, and figured in the concert given
by the students who were leaving the Conservatoire,
which was arranged for the anniversary of Liszt's
birth, the 22nd October, but postponed until the
29th February. It took place at the Budapest

EARLY YEARS 31

Opera, under the direction of István Kerner. According to an article by Zoltán Kodály[1] this Scherzo was a fragment of a symphony. "Koessler advised him to give up composing for a period. Evidently he was at a loss to direct him. Later they collaborated uneasily. Instead of being corrected, the symphony of 1902 has disappeared. Only the scherzo remains to us. It is possible that the project exceeded his technical powers at that time. It is certain that Bartók's progress was halted, and that Koessler was not the man who could aid him."

The main work of this period was the *Kossuth Symphony*. The term was applied doubtless because of the traditional division into four movements; Bartók himself referred to it as a symphonic poem. From the first volume of his correspondence edited by János Demény we can follow his reactions while this work was in hand.

He writes in the autumn of 1902 to his mother: "Went to-day to Professor Thomán. It was his musical day. Apart from many relatives, Madame Gruber was there, Madame Széchy and some others. I played two movements of my symphony. Both were well received, particularly the Scherzo. I was praised for the beauty of the compositions and the excellence of my playing. This last point interested Thomán as a pianist. To-day I also took the slow movement to Koessler, who said to me, 'You must have love in an adagio, but in this

---

[1] "Bartók and Folklore". *Uj Zenei Szemle*—"The New Musical Review." Budapest. 5th October, 1950.

movement there is nothing which speaks of love.
A pity—one of the awkwardnesses of modern
musicians is that they have lost the knack of writing
adagios; that is why they avoid them as much as
they can.' What cannot be demanded of others
cannot be demanded of me. That is why I cannot
but go on with the symphony. If nothing better
comes, the movement can stay as it is, although
one cannot say that it is a success. It is well known
that Koessler is very strict when it comes to judging
an adagio. He has the habit of saying: 'You must
have lived, in order to write an adagio'. Have
lived what? Apparently Love, and all that goes
with it, disappointment, ecstasy, suffering and so
forth. That Life has an influence on the quality of
musical composition I do not believe. I have lived
in all sorts of ways, I also have talent—at least so
they say—so according to this principle I ought to
be able to write a good adagio. For that matter.
Koessler finds that even Dohnányi's adagios are
not impeccable. So do I."

On the 17th January, 1903, he wrote: "I have
had to scribble a lot lately. I have written out
again the fourth movement of the symphony in
order to show it to-day to Koessler. I have already
played it to Madame Gruber, whom it did not
please so much at the first hearing as at the second.
She told me that I have made a good deal of progress since the first movement, and that, after the
scherzo, this pleased her most. Koessler himself
was not so generous in his praises; he made all sorts

of criticisms, but as we had very little time, he criticized a part, not the whole."

On the 18th June, 1903, the score of the *Kossuth* was finished in a form which could be played on the piano. "Koessler has heard my *Kossuth Symphony*, and has pronounced it good on the whole. He wishes me to orchestrate it during the holidays, and then he will present it at the Conservatoire concert. That suits me." After this, Bartók paid his farewell visits to his masters at the Conservatoire. He left the Conservatoire endowed with all the due diplomas, but without having passed any examination which would serve to establish his reputations as a virtuoso and composer. He wrote to his mother, 25th May, 1903, "To the greatest wonder of my fellows I was not required to undergo even the smallest examination, all the authorities agreed there was no point to it."

The orchestration of such an ambitious work could not but be taxing. He was going that year to Gműnden, a fashionable holiday resort in Upper Austria, where Ernst Dohnányi, who was about to marry, and Hans Koessler were spending their vacations and therefore could be depended on for advice. He went first to his family in Poszony, where his mother and sister devotedly copied out the piano score of the *Kossuth Symphony*, while he set himself to the orchestration. He arrived at Gműnden in the first days of August. Then began a period of ease, in artistic and cultivated surroundings—social and friendly meals, walks, receptions,

C

and informal concerts—but it was also a period of work. He wrote to his mother, 23rd August, 1903: "Yesterday I took Koessler the score; and he assured me it was first rate, that it was orchestrated quite in the modern style, and that it would sound magnificent. I have had some difficulty in getting this letter written. Above all I have had so little time, because of so many invitations, and now I am getting down to the slow movement of the Sonata for Violin, which bothers me." Perhaps he was referring to the revised version of the andante which Koessler had prompted, Koessler who had shown himself so difficult in the matter of an adagio.

When the orchestration of the *Kossuth Symphony* was completed, Dohnányi and Bartók went through it together. He wrote to his mother, 1st September, 1903: "I played my Kossuth Symphony to Dohnányi to-day. He said it was good enough, but expressed a thousand and one objections, most of them about details of little significance, that is to say, most of them did not bear on pure music. For example, he thought the introduction of the *Gott Erhalte*,[1] not sufficiently emphatic or not sufficiently caricatured, and so forth. Good, but that is only a detail. Everybody can differ about that. What is important is the competent advice which eventually will sway the majority. True, Dohnányi said again, 'Ah well, Strauss could have orchestrated that'. "

In a later letter, 8th September, he wrote, "My symphony Dohnányi finds pleasant all the same—

---

[1] The Austrian Imperial hymn.

but what pains it took me to discover the fact. He repeated that the best part was the end. Doubtless because one may then hope that it will suddenly come to a stop. Above all, because there the orchestration is more subtle. But he does not act the Maestro." One can well imagine that Dohnányi was not without some jealousy, a recognized master but of too short a standing for him to feel assured. Bartók's mother scented this, for he replied to her, 23rd September, 1903, from Gműnden: "Really you you are mistaken about Dohnányi. I have a great opinion of him, both as a man and as an artist. He is quite without any streak of ill will. As an artist, he is over-severe towards his fellows, but that is not an enormous fault. A greater fault, and an unpardonable one, is his lack of patriotism. That is what has always ruled out good relations between us." There was certainly a fundamental musical opposition between Ernst von Dohnányi and Béla Bartók; the first was an aristocrat, a follower of Brahms, devoted to subtle orchestration; the second a peasant, a post-Wagnerian romantic, set on violent orchestration.

On the 23rd September, 1903, Bartók had some good news for Lajos Dietl: "I do not know whether I told you in my last letter that the Budapest Philharmonic has agreed to produce my *Kossuth*. I am very happy, how good to hear the first performance of my work in Hungary on the 13th January, 1904." The rehearsals were rather stormy, for the instrumentalists of the orchestra, most of them non-

Hungarian, tumbled to the anti-government persuasions of the work and its elements of caricature. Among the brass one of the trumpets refused to play the mangled hymn of Haydn, *Gott Erhalte*, a deformation which was symbolic of the defeat and rout of the Austrians in the Revolution of '48.

The *Kossuth Symphony* was certainly in the style of Strauss, it followed a descriptive plan, its instrumentation was as fresh. Moreover, as in Strauss's symphonic poems, each of the sections of the *Kossuth* illustrated an historical or psychological phase. For instance, in the final movement, Kossuth brusquely awakes at the word, "Press on to the Fight, Come, Come, fine Hungarian knights, young Heroes of Hungary!"

The work was variously received. Bartók himself wrote in his *Curriculum Vitae Succinct*: "A great success. Zoltán Kodály says that the work was too original to please most, though people of taste found it impressive; it threw down the gauntlet of national music, a problem then so discussed, and announced a coming solution."[1] It was performed by the Hallé Orchestra, the conductor being Hans Richter, at Manchester in the presence of Bartók a few weeks after its first performance in Budapest. He wrote to his mother, 1st September, 1904: "I told you I was sending on the Manchester criticisms. Unfortunately, I have lost them on my journey. A pity, because they contained some remarks much to the point." The appearance of this work marks a

---

[1] *Revue Musicale*, March, 1921.

memorable date in Bartók's career, though it still remains in manuscript, and is now never played through; only the Scherzo is sometimes heard.

BARTÓK'S NATIONALISM

THE *Kossuth Symphony* showed there was a force at work in his life no less important than music: this was his ardent patriotism. It is said that he belonged to the Black Tulip, a secret society of Hungarian patriots, but no proof is forthcoming; all that his correspondence shows is that he used every opportunity in speech and in writing to make his position clear. He wrote to his mother in the autumn of 1902: "If only Hungarians would fight harder against the tyranny of the Austrian Army. Nobody goes to the Conservatoire against his will, whereas everybody is forced into the Army and the German language is imposed on all. It is a shame. One can and ought to change things." And again, 12th June, 1903. "The ministers dare to defend the existing army, because it embodies the will of him whom they call King of Hungary! There is no longer a King of Hungary! King of Hungary indeed! Only a Hungarian can be that."

Even student outings were used as occasions for the display of Magyar feeling, which was irritating to the authorities, who were worried by the popular agitation and angered by the obstructive tactics of nationalist Members in Parliament. He wrote:

"For the moment we are not allowed to go to the
Opera. The directors have closed two boxes, because
the students presented Madame Abrányi (a favourite
singer of the nationalists) with a wreath of flowers.
She remains at the Opera. I do not know how the
affair will finish. It is a funny business."

Such excerpts could be written off merely as gusts
of temper, but not since the discovery of a letter
from Gmünden, 8th September, 1903, which shows
what a deliberate nationalist he was. "No news
to speak of for the moment. All that I can
write is a political dissertation about the cause
of Hungarian decadence. It is not, as Dohnányi
says, the fact that the Army's language and spirit
is not Hungarian. Rather, it is the shocking in-
difference to Hungarian matters shown by members
of our nation, with very few exceptions. Not in
matters of high politics, there we can work ourselves up for our national ideals, but in the trivial
things of everyday life, that is where we sin against
the Hungarian nation. 'We care nothing whether
we speak Hungarian, or how we speak it,' said Jenő
Rakosi in an excellent speech, 'We speak any other
language in the world. Anybody who knows only
Hungarian we tax with lack of culture, even if he
has every science in his head; from their tenderest
years we spoil our daughters, mothers of the future
generation; by giving them a foreign education.' He
spoke with reason, for this is what we Hungarians
do, instead of taking every means to foster our
mother tongue. Only so can we be strong, at least

at home. But of course it is as easy for us to speak German as Hungarian (and we are even proud of it) or to buy Austrian as Hungarian goods. Everybody when he grows up should decide for what ideal he wishes to fight, and rule his actions by that end. As regards myself, my whole life, in every field, always and in every way, is at the service of one supreme purpose, the good of the Hungarian nation and fatherland. I believe I have ever given proof of this intention, in small matters as in great, to the best of my poor ability. Unfortunately there is much room for improvement in my very home. I observed with grief, when I was last staying with you, that you and my sister Böske, either from negligence or forgetfulness, commit the very faults I was alluding to. I do not speak of the embarrassment of the upset over the *Gott Erhalte*. That is not of much use to the Hungarian nation: that is a matter for the makers of law and the government, they can put that straight. But not everybody has easy access to a government office, and those who cannot ought to dedicate all their activity, calmly and without parade, in their daily life to all that is Hungarian. One should spread, you must spread, the Hungarian language by what you say, what you do, how you converse. Speak Hungarian among yourselves! ! ! How embarrassed I should be if one of my friends who knew my views should pay a visit to us at Pozsony, or later at Budapest, and should hear you thoughtlessly speaking German among yourselves, or even addressing me in German. He would take me for a hypocrite. You allege that you are in the habit of speaking German with Aunt Irma. The excuse one may accept, yet at the same time it is the result of carelessness past repair. Why did you not get into the way of speaking Hungarian from your youth? Aunt Irma lived a long time in the district of Békés: she learnt our language tolerably well, and you could continue to teach her. If you acquired the habit of speaking German with us in order to teach us that language, you could well have spoken Hungarian with Aunt Irma in order to teach her.

"But I am speaking here beside the point. Because it is obligatory for everybody in Hungary to speak German, that does not make it wrong to speak Hungarian.

"Listen to this, which I address to all Hungarians:

"Do not speak a foreign language except when it is absolutely indispensable. In other words I desire that although you speak another tongue with Aunt Irma you speak nothing else but Hungarian with Böske, inside the house and outside the house, whether I am there or not. 'It is hard to get into it'—then you must rough it, the Hungarian language is worth the trouble.

"And as for speaking a word to me in German, even in joke, that I forbid you. You know my custom, when in shops and in the street, somebody asks me the way in a foreign tongue, I answer in Hungarian. I want you to copy me. 'It is difficult,' but you must conquer the first difficulty, and then it will become easier. I myself have become quite accustomed. It will be sad if my dearest ones do not work for the same end as I do. As regards your old acquaintances, who do not know Hungarian well, you can use your own judgement. But with the Biermanns, and the F's ??!! How often have I noticed that when the conversation is in Hungarian, suddenly you change over to German, by pure inadvertence, because it is all the same to you. That you nickname my sister Böske, or something of the sort, that is not so very important, one may get out of it. But what I have spoken about to-day, and what I now ask of you, that you must do."

What an unbending and determined tone and temper, though these words are softened, for they are addressed to the person Bartók loved best in the world, his mother whom he refused to leave even though it meant remaining under the Nazi menace which he hated. He was to write to Madame Müller, 13th April, 1938,[1]: "And then there is my mother; to leave her for good, for the remaining years of her life, no, that is impossible." In fact, he did not leave Hungary for good until after the death of his mother in 1940.

This love of liberty filled Bartók with a detestation of the cultivated circles which conformed to the prevailing vogue. He preferred the patriarchal life in the countryside. He declared that the happiest days of his life were spent among the peasants. His sense of political freedom ran alongside his sense of

---

[1] Published in the *Uj Zenei Szemle*, 5th October, 1950.

musical freedom; the artist's devotion to folklore
fostered his patriotism. To collect and edit a
national song was a declaration of love for one's
country, a protest against its subjection. The same
thing has happened in other occupied countries;
national sentiment has been kept alive by songs,
more or less intact, depending on the vigilance
of the oppressors: the earliest examples are found
among mountain peoples on invasion routes, for
instance in Bulgaria, Georgia, and in Transylvania which Bartók explored.

From the spirit of liberty came his pointed
criticism. His judgement was rapid, brief, concise,
sharp, prepared to cut and dissect even himself
when it turned inward. His scrupulous mind was
torn with doubts. So he was led to examine fresh
musical tendencies, to experiment with new techniques, however eccentric and strange they might
be, and that without muddling himself or blurring
his own lines of development. His rationalism left no
field unexplored. When he was twenty-five years
old he gave up religion for atheism, or at least for a
certain stoical agnosticism. In 1907, he wrote from
Vésztő (where Bartók often stayed with his sister
Elizabeth, who had married the steward of a country
estate) to Stefi Geyer, who was still his correspon-
dent forty years later:

"After an easy-going opening you suddenly
raise a grave problem. You have not done this
before, though I should have expected it. We must go
into the matter one day, though I am pleased that,

as always, I did not take the first step. I am quite certain, as certain as I was before the matter was raised, that you are a believer. To come to this conclusion is no struggle, what I find more difficult is to talk about it.

"After having reflected for a long time I have come to terms with myself, and can set out my conclusions in order.

"The Bible steadily proclaims what is contrary to ordinary earthly truth: in fact, it is not God who has created man to his own image and likeness, but man who has so created God. So also, it is not true that the soul is immortal and the body mortal, but that the soul disappears while the body, that is matter, goes on for ever. Why should we be taught empty lies? Most people will remain convinced to the day of their death, while the minority will free themselves by a painful struggle which could have been avoided. What is the use of it? How much better if we were taught nothing at all. Much easier to cultivate virgin soil than a waste covered with weeds.

"This fight is part of the universal scheme of things, I have thrown myself into it by degrees. Until I was fourteen years old, I was an ardent Catholic, full of respect for authority. My lively heart reacted against the invasion of secularism; I took the introduction of civil marriage as an attack on the Church's power. Between the ages of fifteen and sixteen my class subjects were religious doctrine, moral theology, ceremonial, dogma, Church History, and anything else that the teachers' zeal added to the curriculum. You cannot imagine how close was our discussion on details. For example, during moral theology, we would take a problem such as the following: if you were struggling in the water with your wife and parents, who according to the laws of the Church should you try to save first? We also learnt the significant point that he who has received the Bishop's permission to eat meat on a Friday cannot eat fish while this permission is in force. We learnt also various manifestations of the Church's gentleness, for instance that nobody has the right to receive a heretic into his house or give him anything to eat, under penalty of excommunication. A heretic, such as I am at present. The most striking result of my teachers' efforts was that from that time forth I ceased in principle to be a Catholic. Not that I settled such questions as 'God' and the 'immortality of the soul'. There I did not advance an inch, I had to wait until I was eighteen when, freed from the scholastic yoke, I could read more serious books. Later, I was much affected by studying astronomy, also by the writings of a Dane, a friend of mine. When I reached the age of twenty-three, I was a new man—an atheist. But I was following what others had thought, for as I read some months ago in an ancient author there is nothing new under the sun.

"Then it was that I eagerly got down to atheistic writings. But now all that seems very dated; and if godless books now fall into my hands I push them aside with distaste. Why should we pile proof on proof—all that we know has been known for centuries. It is childishness, to talk as though I were an atheist merely of four years standing.

"You have often brought up the fact that you lack experience, and now you say that you are not a philosopher. But religion is nothing but pure philosophy. The effort to solve, and only by fumbling in the dark, certain questions which ordinary experience and common sense cannot answer, that is philosophy. What is more natural than for us to meet paradoxes with fantastic affirmations, some more interesting than others, all more or less extraordinary.

"Since you have had no 'serious experience', while I, without having had much, have nevertheless had a little, and since you are not a philosopher while I have dabbled in philosophy, allow me to explain.

"Examine the history of mythologies, and you will see what I mean. The Greeks offered us gods of flesh and blood, who act and suffer as we do. That is why their mythology is much more attractive and artistically congenial than that of the Jews. In the Old Testament the figure of Jehovah is dark and cloudy, but is nevertheless anthropomorphic. He revenges, rewards, punishes—but these are attributes entirely opposed to the notion of the Eternal. The Blessed Trinity of the Christian mythology is more mystical still; it is a dogma which holds the reason in bondage—miserable man, you cannot comprehend, so do not speculate, for speculation here is a mortal

sin. What marvellous progress! It is this that explains
the unmitigated obscurantism of the Middle Ages,
and the sufferings we have had to undergo to be
delivered from it. But this heap of mysticism was
not created by Jesus, who in historic fact was only a
moral teacher, who as such left us one of the
greatest works, though there are points in his
teaching which shock us.

"Nowadays the fashion is an incorporeal spirit,
eternal and omnipresent, whose will rules and has
always ruled everything about us. What an
astonishing mixture of finite and infinite concepts.
His will is finite and settled—how then can we
attribute that to an infinite spirit?

"All this, besides, is supposition based on the
existence of the universe. We say: look, the world is
an organic whole—it is impossible that alone it
formed itself, for nothing makes itself. And the
confusion grows when we consider that the world is
governed throughout according to a marvellously
harmonious order. Hence, it must have been
created by a being of such and such a sort—in
fact, all manner of different definitions are advanced.
He has neither arms, legs, head—but he thinks and
wills. Again, we are faced with an indescribable
muddle. For we are bound to say that thinking and
willing are functions of the brain, and nothing else,
and that without brain there is no thinking or
willing. How a being without a brain can think or
will is quite inconceivable; even the possibility of
one is undemonstrable, but if we speak of it as an

hypothesis, let us at least speak of its applications so as to avoid mistakes.

"It is a gross error to form rash theories about the origin and existence of the world. If I do not know how such or such an object has been transported into a container which I have closed and locked up myself, why should I then be obliged to invent a fairy tale to the effect that since it is impossible to discover how it got there, and since the whole affair is inconveivable, it is certain that so-and-so put it there? That is an impossible line of reasoning. Yet that is how we go on about the world. Why not simply say: 'I just cannot explain the reason for its presence, and that is all'?

"Who is the man who knows, or may one day know, the whole world? There is no such man! For the world is infinite in space and time. A finite brain can never conquer the infinite. In planetary space, we can traverse a hundred and thirty light years, and we can analyse the chemical composition and calculate the movements of the stars that distance away. But what is that in comparison with the infinite? How can we determine the origin of such an unknowable reality, or even try to measure the world? Here we must stop, fold our hands, and avow our complete impotence. Our desire to know allows us to know a little about space and time, but that is nothing in comparison with the whole. We have no right even to discuss it; all we can do is to advance hypotheses about the origin of the existence of something about which we know nothing.

"But man is proud and will not bow his head. Not only does he stand up against the infinite, bravely, or rather rashly, but he even appropriates to himself some part of it. The soul is immortal, he affirms. We need not now strive to settle what is meant by soul, but merely to discover the sense of the proposition which says that what we call soul is immortal. That signifies, does it not, that the soul is infinite, but only in a certain sense. Only when looking forward, not in looking back, for everybody must say that the soul begins only when man is born. Is it possible to imagine how a being can be infinite in one way and not in another? That is, I think, a reason why the proof neither could nor should be attempted. That is self-evident, a sure axiom and one of the principal proofs of the soul's mortality.

"But let us suppose that the soul is immortal. What vexing questions then crop up. They are important, yet nevertheless insoluble. Where, and when, does the soul begin? When does that immortal being begin? In the child, or before birth in the mother's womb? And if so, at what stage? Or if during birth, at what moment? Or after birth, then at what age? Yet it is surely important to know if a baby who dies when two weeks old, or a still-born child, has had a soul, or whether a pregnant woman carries within her one soul or two!

"If we treat the soul as an immortal spirit, then we cannot measure it with the instruments of physical science, and we cannot answer these questions.

"And where does the soul begin? Why should a two-weeks old baby have a soul more than an animal with a more developed brain, for the latter shows greater intelligence than a little slip of a human? Why should an idiot, an imbecile from birth, have more soul than an intelligent animal does? To this, quite a lot of women reply that animals certainly do have souls. But how can that be? For then there would be souls in snakes, snails, earthworms.

"And why not also amoeba, infusoria, microbes and bacilli? And then, if we cross the frontier into the vegetable order, perhaps plants also have souls, and even stones. Thus, these improvised questions do not throw much light on the matter. And yet, we must draw the line somewhere, if the soul is immortal, and we should be able to certify beyond question whether this or that is soul or vapour, immortal or not.

"What is the soul? The functioning of the brain and nervous centres, which develops slowly, from before birth, and corresponds to the appropriate organs and does not completely stop until the moment of death. What comes then to an end is mortal. But the body as matter is immortal, for matter is indestructible; it is not lost to the world, but only changes its form.

"The belief in gods rises in the first place from human weakness. At the beginning, man considered every object of which he was not the absolute master as a being endowed with mind and will from which

D

he must obtain favours. He made a little god of
each one. But there were so many of them that they
could not be counted. This was embarrassing, so on
reflection, he cut down their number and grouped
them around certain definite principles. So men
passed from pantheism to polytheism, then to
monotheism, then to atheism. Each new theory
effaced the preceding one. This explains the easy
victory of Christianity, with its sublime morality,
over the rotting forms of Greek and Roman polytheism. Yet, quite clearly, Christianity in decay
cannot repeat the victory.

"That man in his misery finds precious comfort
in praying to an omnipotent Being is under-
standable. He may receive in return a crumb of
bread, a drop of water. But how unspeakably
feeble! And what shall we say of other recompenses
from aloft, of the punishment of those who do evil?
All these are very human formulae, their significance is not that they are true, but that they are a
comfort to those who suffer. Perhaps that is why
many particularly intelligent priests appear to
believe—for the sake of those who would despair if
they lost their faith, which is their last prop.
Others, of course, are merely moved by love of
gain.

"God, God, good God, only a little time back I
would have sought to convert everybody to atheism,
for freedom of thought is the only source of happiness.
Now it is all the same to me: let everybody do as he
likes. Though it is a bore if believers attack me and

invoke legal sanctions to compel me to public manifestations of religion.

"Oh, I wish I had not dealt with the question in this manner, but instead in sweet and melancholy tones, without discord. And now, I find my pen has run away with me. The kingdom of discord, that is mine!

"You asked me to write on this subject, and I beg of you not to be upset with me, or think of me otherwise than as before. Above all, I beg you, do not be sorry for me, any regrets will hurt me. You will comment, I hope, on my long exposition. How? By letter, or in person? Are the ten or a dozen kilometres which separate us too great a distance for us to write to one another? However, if you write, do choose a time when you do not have to go and visit your cousin and when your letter will not have to be cut down by three-quarters. . . .

". . . A few further remarks on the subject of the purpose of life. I speak of the absolute purpose, not the relative. For certainly, in its modest way, everything has a purpose, even the mosquito and the flea. As regards myself, I desire a little happiness for a few—to serve the society of run-to-seed princelings called the Hungarian intelligentsia by collecting national songs and so forth. And my reward will be some bread, and the inclusion of my name in the next edition of *Who's Who*, which will enable any strummer to find me the more easily if he wants a recommendation to the

35648

Academy. The purpose and the reward of life are about equally impressive.

"But it is not about that that I want to speak. Terrestrial life one day began, and one day will end. Our astronomers can already calculate when this will take place—millions of years ahead, but tragic anyhow for us men, who cheerfully construct hypotheses about the ending of it all. But the manner matters little; the point is that it will certainly happen one day. But well before that, there will be radical changes in the social order, in ways of thinking, in taste and sensibility. What we now hold in honour will then be little thought of, and contrariwise. It is certain that in a thousand years, or in ten thousand years, no trace of my work will survive. Perhaps the Hungarian people and the Hungarian language will be forgotten and never more remembered. If not then, then later on. It is the fate that overtakes us all. But it is not very agreeable to work with this sad thought. We should rejoice in life, and be interested in everything that goes on in the world around us. One should be enthusiastic about the Trinity of which you have spoken so gracefully. Were I to make the sign of the Cross, I would say, 'In the name of Nature, of Art, and of Science'.

"Isn't that enough? Or must you have the additional promise of a world to come? That I do not understand. But it should not impede an epistolary friendship. How can we arrange that?

"You are not a philosopher. What does that matter; you have but to want to be one.

"You are still green? What does it matter; you have but to want to grow. Anyhow, you are not so very green!

"Will you allow me to send you books from time to time? Not too difficult ones, to begin with, but no compromises!

"Even if they give you some grey hairs, they will give you much joy in exchange.

"Think of the Infinite. Tremble and bow your head before him.

"Friendly greetings from an atheist—who is much more honest than the majority of believers."[1]

BARTÓK'S ENTRY INTO PUBLIC LIFE

THE Liszt bursary which he gained in 1903 relieved Bartók of certain financial difficulties and enabled him to take up residence in Berlin. Here, there was nothing that did not delight him: concerts, operas perfectly produced, wonderful conductors— he was struck especially by Weingartner—a rich musical life, and a well organized musical library offered everything that could satisfy the curiosity of such an eager young artist. But above all, this bursary bestowed on him the most precious of all gifts for the man who must earn his living through

---

[1] The letter was published in the *Uj Zenei Szemle*, October, 1950.

NAZARETH COLLEGE
LIBRARY

creative activity: time. He therefore set to work on
an important composition for piano and orchestra
in which he intended to wed his urgent need to
express himself as an artist to his equally urgent need
to earn his living as a performer. With this work,
he hoped to display himself to the public in his dual
role of virtuoso and composer, and perhaps, while
obtaining some honourable publicity in the first
role, to establish himself as a master in the second.
This work, the *Rhapsody for Piano and Orchestra*, was
finished towards the end of 1904. It is a key work,
marking the end of what may be called Bartók's
preparatory period, for in its pages—now dreamily
poetic and now full of exuberant czardas, free and
yet full of a Lisztian shapeliness—Bartók moves
from the field of international to that of national
music. Soon he is to dive deep into the folk music of
the Magyars. It was with this composition that
Bartók competed in Paris, in July of 1905, in the
Anton Rubinstein International Competition for
composition and playing.

Bartók arrived in Paris bringing with him not
only the *Rhapsody* but the *Quintet* and the *Violin
Sonata*. He stayed at Madame Condat's *pension* in
the Rue Clément Marot. His fellow boarders were a
cosmopolitan set: there were twenty of them, including North and South Americans, Cubans,
Dutchmen, Spaniards and Englishmen. Bartók
liked the place, for Madame Condat was specially
considerate and took a personal interest in him. He
needed such sympathy, for he was unsuccessful in

the competition, and the violence with which he expressed his fury at this failure was not, in itself, enough to console him.

Early in August, 1905, he wrote to his mother: "I am sorry to tell you that I had no success at the competition. There is nothing remarkable in the fact that I failed to win a prize for my piano playing, and no reason to be annoyed. What is really disgusting is the way the prize for composition was awarded—or, rather, was *not* awarded. Dietl, who was on the jury, gave me a detailed account of the affair. There were five candidates, and while the jury was deliberating, the following questions were asked: 1. Must we give the first prize? (Two for, thirteen against); 2. Must we give the second prize? (Five for, ten against); 3. If we do not give any prizes, must we give honourable mentions? (Ten for, five against); 4. In that case, to whom should we give them? (Brugnoli was given ten votes, Bartók nine, Flament two, Weinberg one, each member of the jury being allowed to put forward two or three names).

"Brugnoli thus had the first honourable mention, while Flament and Weinberg naturally received no mention at all. I am going to send my diploma of (dis-)honour back to Auer in St. Petersburg. I will not stand for such asinine behaviour.

"All the same, my pieces were quite well played. The really shocking thing is that, even so, the jury did not understand them. And then, I ran into so much hostility! I almost had to withdraw my candidature. By way of greeting me, they told me that the various movements of the *Rhapsody* were full of faults, that the whole work was extremely difficult, that there was not enough time for rehearsals, that, in short, it could not be played. I corrected the parts (there were perhaps ten or a dozen errors in all), and in spite of all these vexations, the final performance was not at all bad.

"As to the *Quintet* they told me flatly and categorically that they could not study it, for they hadn't enough time. Happily, I had the *Violin Sonata* with me (though whether I had it or not, didn't in the end really matter), and this they were willing to play. How much time it took to get a violinist! Finally a young Russian, a pupil of Auer's, called Zeitlin, rehearsed it with me and played it. Thus I had prepared my second copy of the *Quintet* all to no purpose (in view of the extraordinary circumstances, they dispensed with a second copy of the *Sonata*.) Nobody looked over the transcription for piano of the orchestral accompaniment of the *Rhapsody*; and that had taken me six hours of work. Why those empty-headed morons of St. Petersburg demanded *that* is really beyond my comprehension.

"The four other composers had brought along things totally lacking in interest. Brugnoli's pieces had at least a certain outward show about them. Ságody's piece was really beyond belief; the public very nearly burst out laughing when it was played; it was such sheer idiocy.

"I have had successes of several kinds with the larger public. Three young men asked me, first in French, then in English, if my *Sonata* had been published! They wanted to buy it. Several people have expressed their lively approval of my work to me. The young Russian, Zeitlin, was quite carried away. He is leaving to take up a post as a conductor in Helsinki in a month. He has asked me for a copy of the *Sonata* when it appears, he would like to play it there. He consoled me by telling me that there were many Russians on the jury, and that in Russia people are not yet used to this kind of music, they still play hardly anything there but Haydn, Mozart, and Beethoven.

"If at least some fairly decent composer had got the prize instead of me, I would say nothing. But that these beasts should have said that my works were unworthy of the prize shows a quite unheard-of degree of stupidity.

"Perger, in the first place, simply failed to understand me. Auer said: '*Ja, das ist die neue Schule, wir sind schon zu alt für so etwas*' ('Yes, that's the new school, we're too old for it'). Chevillard, the famous French conductor, who was also on the jury, said that it was 'very interesting'. Holländer, the Berlin violinist, also liked it; he wants to play my *Violin Sonata* with me, and perhaps the 'famous *Quintet*' in Berlin . . .

"My landlady, Madame Condat, also came to the competition. She is disgusted, and in her rage with the jury has brought down the price of my room

from nine to seven francs. It's really very cheap.
My money will still last a month." (He needed ten
francs a day.)

Happily, there was still Paris to console him,
wonderful in its unique diversity, so full of distrac-
tions and of peace, rich, gay and noble, a town of
pleasure and a city of art.

He wrote to Irmy Jurkovics, 15th August, 1905:
"One thing consoles me, that I have been able to
come to Paris, that divine and godless city. It
cannot be described, you have to see all the lovely
things—and how lovely!—gathered together here, at
the centre of the world. With what art Paris is
built! Vienna and Berlin are nothing in comparison!
(I still have some hopes for Budapest, although it
lacks the irreplaceable ancient monuments) . . .

". . . But what a joy, when one visits a museum, to
encounter one after the other the masterpieces one
knows so well in reproductions—the Mona Lisa, the
madonnas of Raphael, the portraits of Madame
Vigée-Lebrun, Murillo's young beggar, and so on.
I can honestly say that hardly any painting has ever
affected me so much as Murillo's big canvases in
the Louvre. Leaving aside all their other perfec-
tions, of which one can get some notion from
reproductions, the harmony of colour in these
pictures has a magical quality such as no other
painter has succeeded in capturing. I set it mentally
beside my 'impressions' at hearing *Tristan* and
Zarathustra at Weingartner's first concert in Berlin,
or at the Dohnányi-Beethoven concert this year in

Vienna, or at my first glimpse, three or four years ago, of St. Stephen's Cathedral in Vienna.

"Today, I went to see a lot of impressionist paintings at the Luxembourg."

But the young man's explorations did not stop there. He visited Montmartre, the Place Pigalle, the Moulin Rouge, the Cabaret du Néant, the Eiffel Tower, and even—by one of the so-called "pleasure trains" of the years before the first world war—Dieppe. Everything aroused his enthusiasm—everything, that is, except French music.

To Madame Jurkovics, he wrote: "In reply to your letter, I must say outright that Bach, Beethoven, Schubert and Wagner have imbued their music with such a strong character that, beside it, the whole mass of French, Italian and Slav music is mere trifling! Liszt gets nearest to the four great masters, but he rarely writes as a Hungarian."

It is amusing to hear Bartók advancing such an opinion, since we know with what veneration he was later to regard French music. In 1907, he was to say that French music had been to him what the vision on the road to Damascus was to St. Paul!

CHAPTER TWO

BARTÓK AND FOLK-MUSIC

THE MOMENT has arrived to examine Bartók's use of folk-music—for this theme will crop up whenever we have to discuss Bartók's harmonies, his form, or his style. Explicitly or implicitly, folk-music underlies all his work. Bartók formally acknowledges the fact when, in his autobiography, he reaches the year 1905: for it was in that year that Zoltán Kodály initiated him into the technique of collecting folk-music.

"In 1905," he writes, "I started out on a search for Hungarian peasant melodies, which were then virtually unknown. I had the good luck to find an excellent collaborator in Zoltán Kodály, who, with his perspicacity and critical sense, gave me invaluable advice in all branches of music. I began my researches from a purely musical point of view, restricting myself to Hungarian-speaking territory. Later, the musical material collected was scientifically examined, and at the same time, I extended my activities to the Slovak and Rumanian language territories.

"This whole study of folk-music was of capital importance in enabling me to free myself from the tyranny, which I had up to then accepted, of the major and minor modal systems. In fact, the largest and most valuable part of this treasure-house of collected folk melodies was based on the old liturgical modes, on the archaic Greek mode, or on one more primitive still (the so-called pentatonic). In addition, all this music abounded in rhythmic devices and the most free and varied changes of measure, demanding now a strict *tempo giusto* and now *rubato* treatment. It thus became clear that in this early Hungarian music, there were scales which, though no longer used, had lost none of their vital force. By reviving them, one might create new harmonic combinations. By using the diatonic scale, I was able to free myself from the fixed 'major-minor' convention: and the final result has been that, to-day, one may employ freely and in isolation all the sounds of the dodecaphonic chromatic system.''

Bartók naturally made the study of Magyar popular music his starting point, for it was geographically nearest to hand, and psychologically nearest to the creative impulses of his unconscious mind. And it was these Magyar elements which, almost to the exclusion of other folk-music gathered in other countries, formed the setting in which Bartók's inspiration most often took fire.

MAGYAR FOLK-MUSIC

BARTÓK himself has given a concise description of the different classes and types of Magyar folk-music

in a brief study which he published in the first
number of the *Revue Musicale* (1st November, 1921).
In quoting that article here, however, I have taken
the liberty of putting in a few explanations in
brackets for the sake of readers who are not experts
in musical technique. What should be explained
at once is that, in making a schematic analysis of a
poem or a song, one designates each of its con-
stituent elements by a different letter of the alpha-
bet. Thus: A B A = first idea, second idea, and
return of first idea; and A A¹ B C A = first idea,
variation of first idea, second idea, third idea, and
return to first idea.

"The territories inhabited by those who are
Hungarians by race and not merely by national-
ity," writes Bartók, "are divided into two distinct
and compact regions. One of these regions, the
larger is present-day Hungary, with stretches of
territory inhabited by Magyars that go beyond the
borders fixed by the Treaty of Trianon as far as the
towns of Nyitra, Szatmar and Nagyvárad. The
other region, a much smaller one, is that of Szekely
and Transylvania, with about half a million Magyar
inhabitants, separated from their fellow-Magyars
in the first region by a large Rumanian area. It was
only at the beginning of this century that folklore
experts began to exploit this territory from a musical
point of view. The first man in the field was Béla
Vikár, the well-known writer and student of folklore, who, not being trained in music, was also the
first to use a phonograph to record folk melodies.

In addition Zoltán Kodály, the present writer and two or three other young composers took part in the work, which resulted in the collection of 8,000 melodies, including variants, all still unpublished.

"This body of material can be divided into three groups:

(i) a group which represents the ancient musical style;

(ii) a group of various melodies having no homogeneous style;

(iii) a group which represents the modern style.

"The archaic tonal colour and the *parlando-rubato* rhythm (the free and varied rhythm of a recitative) of the melodies in the ancient style gives us authority to assume that these melodies perhaps represent the remnants of an ancient musical culture still preserved among the peasantry. Their antiquity can be seen above all in the scale which they predominantly employ, which is the pentatonic: G, B-flat, C, D, F, G. The scale can be represented in this fashion, or in such a way that the two sounds of the diatonic scale which initially have no place in it, E-flat and A, or A-flat and E, play a passing role on a weak beat, or as secondary tones in a *grupetto* (a decorative group of sounds rapidly emitted round a principal note). In this case, the scale which was originally pentatonic is transformed into the Dorian mode (the scale of D without accidentals, or its transposition, that is to say a scale comprising the same intervals), the Aeolian

(the scale of A without accidentals, or its transposition), or the Phrygian (the scale of E without
accidentals or its transposition). The structure of
these melodies also bears witness to their age: the
four parts of the melody, called melodic lines—and
corresponding to the four lines of the stanza, where
each line has an equal number of syllables—are,
for the most part, different from each other. Their
construction can thus hardly be called architectonic.
This construction is in direct contrast to the architectonic form of most Western melodies, a superior
form which has evolved in a much more complicated
way. As for the rhythm of these ancient melodies,
one notices immediately that the musical phrase
never begins on a weak beat—which, besides, is
no less characteristic of the other two groups, the
Slovaks and Rumanians. This is directly related
to one of the chief phonetic rules of the Hungarian
language, in which it is always the first syllable of
the word that carries the stress or tonic accent. It
should also be noted, in relation to this *parlando-
rubato* rhythm, that the final notes of any melodic
line prolong themselves in a perceptible manner,
and that some other sounds are adorned with rich
fioriture. In certain melodies in the ancient style, we
find a rigorous dance rhythm, such as is characterized by such a rhythm as:

and at the end of the melodic lines:

"These melodies do not derive from the folk-music of our neighbours. This use of the pentatonic system leads us, rather, to suppose that we have here the remnants of an old musical folk-culture brought from Asia by the first Magyars, a music which has perhaps a direct relationship with the pentatonic music of Tcheremisses, Tatars, and Kirghizes." (Bartók's supposition is all the more plausible because the defective skeletonic scale alluded to has its origins in the Far East. A knowledge of the history of the invasions of Europe, of migrations and of ancient trade routes enabled Bartók and his contemporaries to grasp this relationship.)

"The second group of melodies has no homogeneous style. These melodies seem to have been produced by the transformation of various musical elements imported from abroad, generally from the West. The route of penetration seems to have been from the Germanic lands through those of the Czechs, Moravians and Slovaks. This, at least, would explain why many of these melodies are still to be found among the Slovaks as well as the Magyars. Much of this material bears the mark of Western modes, that of major and minor keys. But another fairly large group of melodies has under-

E

gone a transformation in the atmosphere of Eastern
Europe; they have become fresher, more exotic.
Their rhythm is for the most part *tempo giusto* (the
strict rhythm as opposed to the *parlando-rubato* of
the first group). Their structure is occasionally
architectonic, as for instance A A B A—the pattern
of a short song. The number of syllables in each
line of verse is often different, but in a symmetrical
fashion, with for instance, lines of 8, 6, 8 and 6, or
6, 6, 8 and 6 syllables. It is from the rhythmical
point of view that they are most fascinating. The
influence of Eastern Europe seems to have transformed the original beginning of the phrase
on a weak beat to a beginning on a strong
beat. Moreover, certain rhythmic patterns have
undergone certain changes to suit the musical needs
of the Magyar peasantry. Thus, measures in a 3/4
rhythm are frequent. And the mixture of different
measures in one piece is by no means uncommon."

And now this is what Bartók has to say about
the third group:

"The development of the new style of popular
music dates from the second half of the last century.
It is above all in the construction of the melodies
that it differs from the old style: the structure of the
more modern melodies is almost exclusively architectonic. Alongside such forms as A B B A, A A B A,
there are also very frequently forms such as A A5
B A and A A5 A5 A (where A5 signifies the first
theme, but a fifth higher, that is, on the dominant).
In other words, in these four patterns, the first and

last lines are identical, which gives them a solidly finished architectonic structure. Their rhythm is, almost exclusively, the strict rhythm of the dance, derived, with certain developments, from the *tempo giusto* of the ancient style. In regard to the melodic line, in certain types of melody in the Dorian or Aeolian mode, we can easily discover the influence of the old pentatonic scale. Nevertheless, the Western major mode can already be found in a great number of them. The Mixolydian mode (the scale of G without accidentals, or its transposition) is not rare either. The Phrygian is, however, less frequent, and the Lydian mode (the scale of F, or its transposition), which is so characteristic of some Slovak melodies, has no place in any of the three groups.

"Certainly there is much charm and freshness in these recent products of Hungarian popular music: but if we have to consider their merit by comparison with the old popular music, we cannot fail to prefer the latter, because of its grave melodies with their rich, penetrating melancholy. Musicians find a far greater stimulus to their creative imagination in the old music, with its rare and exquisite reserve, than in the easy and accessible gaiety of the modern folk-music. . . . Yet, thanks to this modern style, there has been a rich flowering of new melodies among the Slovaks and the Ruthenians, of melodies perceptibly different from their Magyar models, the first germs, perhaps, of a new musical style which is in process of formation. . . ."

AN ELEMENT OF DECADENCE: GYPSY MUSIC

To summarize in less technical language the
distortions produced by foreign influences of which
Bartók has just been speaking, we can perhaps
say that under the German influence, Hungarian
folk songs and dances accepted the simple, regular
rhythms of Western music, and their modality took
on a colouring of tonality. The gypsy style, for its
part, produced a greater use of *rubatos* and an
efflorescence of ornaments and *fioriture* in the Italian
style, thus disfiguring the noble lines of the archaic
melody and facilitating the erosive advance of
expressionism.

It was this last influence above all which was
catastrophic. At the end of his article, Bartók
explains how it entered the picture: "Formerly,
in Hungary, the village musician was always a
peasant. According to what region he came from,
his usual instrument was the bagpipe, the primitive
hurdy-gurdy, or the rustic flute. He was engaged
for Sunday dances, for weddings, and other village
celebrations, and although he was paid for his
services, this was simply an extra source of money
for him, since his main job was always that of a
tiller of the soil. Little by little, however, this
lucrative post of village musician seems to have
passed into the hands of the Gypsies, not only
among the Magyars, but among the Slovaks and
Ruthenians. It appears that, in the old days, the

Gypsies performed exclusively for the country squires; it was only later that they penetrated among the peasants, who were always readily susceptible to the charm of aristocratic ways. However this may be, it is certainly true that the Gypsies always played what their clients wanted: to the nobility they played melodies written or chosen by aristocratic dilettantes, and to the peasants, country tunes. But if the audience made no objection, they were quite prepared to run through their entire repertoire. And in this way, they spread among the peasantry the melodies of noble amateurs. Since they were primarily musicians for the aristocracy, it was only to be expected that they should be saturated with these pseudo-popular airs. At the same time, they worked their own subtle transformations on everything they played."

The appropriation of Hungarian folk-music by the Gypsies became so widespread that it led even Liszt astray, for in his book on Gypsy music he confuses it with genuine Hungarian popular music. Bartók, in the speech he made in tribute to Liszt in 1933, on being received into the Academy, explained the error, and even expressed doubts as to the existence of an authentic Gypsy music.

Alas! Every producer of cabaret, revue or radio feature continues to put out, under the title of "Hungarian music", a flood of songs and dances in the so-called "Gypsy style", whose shameless expressionism can only make a person of taste shudder. There is as much difference between these and authentic Magyar music as between the latest jazz "hit" and a Renaissance air.

COLLECTING FOLK-MUSIC

In a detailed and informative lecture called *Essai d'un code de folklore musical*, Bartók has explained the technique of gathering folk material in the musical field and the qualities that it demands: ". . . in fact, the ideal collector of folk-music should possess really encyclopædic learning. He must have a knowledge of philology and phonetics if he is to notice and record the delicate shades of regional pronunciation; he must be a choreographer, in order to describe with precision the relationships between music and the folk-dance. It is only by means of wide general anthropological knowledge that he can establish the relationship that exists, down to the most apparently insignificant details, between folk-music and folk-customs. He must be enough of a sociologist to calculate the influence upon folk-music of various disturbances in the collective life of the village. If he wants to draw conclusions, he needs historical knowledge, primarily about the movements and settlements of ancient tribes; if he wants to make comparisons with the folk-music of other peoples, he must learn the foreign languages in question. Finally, and above all, he must be a musician with a good ear, and a good observer. An expert in musical folk-lore who unites in himself so many capacities, so much learning and so much practical experience has not, to my knowledge, yet been discovered and perhaps never will be discovered. . . ."

Even more qualities than these are necessary for the successful leader of such voyages of musical exploration. How many difficulties had not Bartók to conquer before he could bring up to the light of civilized day the shining ore of the folk-song! Can we imagine what his travels must have been like, cumbered as they were by recording machines, blank discs, music paper and so many other impedimenta, among the plains and mountains of Hungary, the Balkans, Turkey, and Algeria? Physical resistance, patience, tenacity must be the prime virtues of the musical anthropologist—and one should not forget diplomatic tact. Anybody who has been in the presence of an old woman, the last depositary of some tradition—one of the last branches of a tree of song—must know what prodigies of coaxing are necessary to make her sing; one has, perhaps, to visit her ten times and over a period of several days to obtain a document that represents an unaffected interpretation. The phonograph has certainly made things easier because of the pleasure singers have in hearing an immediate play-back.

To-day, thanks to Bartók's efforts and the new impulse which he gave to musical anthropology by interesting the younger generation in it, more than

16,000 Hungarian folk-songs have been recorded,
hundreds of collections, of which some dozens are
due to Bartók himself, have been published, more
than a thousand monographs on the theme have
also been published in Hungary, and, what is just
as important, work of the same sort has been going
on in neighbouring countries, whose scholars have
been seized by a noble emulation after reading
Bartók's monumental contributions to the science:
Das Ungarische Volkslied, *Chansons Populaires du
Département du Bihar*, *Melodien der Rumänischen Weih-
nachtslieder* (Colindas) and *Volksmusik der Rumänen
von Maramuresch*.

BARTÓK'S TREATMENT OF FOLK-SONGS

ONCE he had completed his collecting of folk-
songs—but only then—Bartók turned to purely
aesthetic considerations.

Around certain melodies he created an atmosphere all his own, by furnishing them with an
accompaniment, by "harmonizing" them. He did
not, however, rest content merely with versions
for voice and piano, but was equally ready to trans-
pose these melodies into much more complicated
instrumental settings, using piano, violin, mixed
choirs, children's choirs and full orchestra.

We can distinguish six periods in his use of folk
material, and they are of progressively increasing
importance.

The first lasted for approximately five years, and ended about 1905. Bartók employed the Lisztian stylization for group songs and dances. The *First Rhapsody for Piano and Orchestra* is a good example.

The second period began immediately after Bartók's meeting in 1905 with Zoltán Kodály, his initiator into the methods of gathering musical folklore. Bartók himself characterized this period in the following words: "We provided the original peasant melody with an accompaniment, but without otherwise altering it, or at most only very slightly, and then set it between a prelude and a postlude. Works of this type bear some analogy to the way in which Bach constructed his chorales." One of the most typical examples of this manner is the collection of eight Magyar popular melodies dating between 1907 and 1917.

The third period was characterized by an extension of the role of harmonization, in which the original melody was given a complex instrumental setting. Here, in fact, we have the first germs of the transition from authentic to imaginary folk-music. The *Sonatina for Piano* (1915) clearly defines this moment of transition.

The fourth period began immediately after the first World War. By now, the transition was complete: a subjective inspiration now filled the originally anonymous popular music, although its first outlines still remained recognizable. Bartók himself explained the matter by saying: "Here the peasant melody has become purely a symbol, and the essential thing is its setting. . . ." But he added: ". . . . the melody and all that we have added to it must give an impression of inseparable unity." The *Improvisations* of 1920 illustrate this phase.

With the fifth period, we enter the realm of "imaginary folk-lore", that extraordinary efflorescence heralded by the cycle of dances known as *Dance Suite*, of 1923. This, in Bartók's own words, was the moment when folk-music "becomes the composer's native language, so that he employs it as freely as the poet does his own native tongue."

And thus, through the alchemy of all these earlier transformations, we reach the sixth period— the period of "pure" music—whose first fruits were the *Fourth Quartet* (1928) and the *Fifth Quartet* (1934), as well as the *Music for Strings, Percussion and Celesta* (1936). It can be seen, then, that for Bartók, pure music was not merely an intellectual structure raised on a simple initial premise, but a sublimation of the popular style, in which the native language of music was raised to the peak of high art. The *Sonata for Two Pianos and Percussion*, of 1937, abundantly proves the point, and serves as a marvellous signpost, besides, to all Bartók's later achievements.

CHAPTER THREE

FROM REAL TO IMAGINARY FOLK-MUSIC

THE INFLEXIBLE line of development which led Bartók logically from real to imaginary folk-music, and then on to pure music, earned him the hostility of a Germanized officialdom, disconcerted the indolent mass of concert-goers, and even bewildered some of his own friends, who were unable to see beyond the charms of authentic folk melodies. Indeed, had he been content to remain at that first stage, his career would doubtless have made much more rapid strides—one has only to look at the great success achieved by the symphonies of Rimsky-Korsakov and Borodin, which owe so much to their use of picturesque folk themes. Having once won his early battles with German academicism, he would have found a large audience readily susceptible to the charms of fantasies, suites and variations on popular melodies.

Bartók understood, however, that while such material could be used for decorative effect, it could never provide him with basic ideas for original works. His problem was to trace back to its source that spring of feeling which country songs and dances had released in him, and thus to rediscover the mechanisms that would allow him to recreate, on his own account, equally compelling melodies and rhythms—to construct, in other words, a sort of personal folk-music, an imaginary folk-music. He sensed that to follow this path was vital to his whole musical future, that through it he would ultimately reach the domain of pure music.

All the same, it was a brave decision to take: for it was a path that he would have to travel alone. The common people whom he loved would not understand him; nor, for that matter, would the majority of his colleagues. The ethnographers for whose work he himself had provided the justification would often speak of him as an "amateur", and other composers whom he would teach as merely a "folklorist". And yet, he stuck to his chosen way, even though often hurt and sometimes reduced to despair by this general lack of understanding.

During the summer of 1905 Bartók composed his first orchestral suite. In its structure it more or less followed the plan of a symphony, but its mood was reflected in a texture full of details obviously inspired by folk melodies. These folk elements were not developed according to the nineteenth-century traditions of technical construction, but were concentrated only on the important sections of the contrapuntal substance. In consequence, their expression had a more restricted, a less generalized air, it smacked less of "pure music" than the symphonic form suggested. In addition, throughout these five movements there is a very definite feeling for nature, expressed by instrumental touches that foreshadow certain impressionist techniques. What, indeed, could one expect in a work of this period, other than allusions to folk melodies, rhythms of folk dances, a sentiment of rusticity: Bartók, carried away by his passion for collecting folk music, had nothing else in his head. In 1906, it even seemed that this passion was going to absorb him totally. His mood is shown in the letter he wrote to his mother on 15th July, 1906, from Vészt (in the county of Békés), the summer villa of Keresztes: "On Sunday, Geza took me into the county of Bihar, to the *puszta* of Fekete-Er, near Sarkad, where I at last found some material. Here I met Franck, who at once asked me to spend a day with him at Doboz. On Monday I went with my machine among the swineherds and the shepherds, and in the afternoon and evening I took recordings from Benedek's maid. On Tuesday morning, as I was leaving, Galgóczy brought a harvester along, then I set off for Doboz.

"The mayor of Fekete-Er sent me an old singer of his, and Franck brought in some singers for dinner, so I was able to make recordings and notes during the evening. In all, in this neighbourhood, I have noted down 83 songs and made 47 recordings. Franck has been very nice; he has invited me for a few weeks in October or November; we can then make excursions to the various estates in the neighbourhood, and explore and prospect the whole region."

This was a happy enthusiasm, but it could easily
have proved fatal, both to the virtuoso and the
composer in Bartók. The following extract from
a letter he wrote to Dietl from Budapest, in November, 1906, clearly illustrates the danger: "For
the moment, the Tulip League is dragging me
by main force to Pressburg. I am to play for
the writers' group there on Sunday, that is to-
morrow." (This, incidentally, is interesting as it
tends to prove that Bartók, if not actually a
member of the Black Tulip, that nationalist society
referred to earlier, was at least closely connected
with it.) "Apponyi and his wife will be there. It's
a great nuisance. I have hardly touched a piano
for six months, so for two weeks now, I've been
forcing my fingers to play the nullities I know by
heart. I had a piano sent to me in Gömör county,
to the famous *puszta* of Gerlice. But to the devil
with exercises! They are the last things I want to
waste my time on. I should have preferred to
collect as many songs as possible. I've already
noted down about one hundred and fifty. . . .

"Come and spend a few days with us at Christmas. We could make a little folk-music prospecting
tour of the neighbouring villages. It's extra-
ordinarily interesting, especially with the phonograph. . . ."

The reader will now readily understand why
Bartók composed nothing during the year 1906.

But the peace of folk museums was not to be
Bartók's fate . . . nor any other sort of peace. For

he was a being of fire and storm—fire and storm directed alternately by his intelligence and his will. . . .

In the autumn of 1906, he sketched out a large-scale work, the *Second Suite for Orchestra*, which he completed in 1907. All four movements bear witness to his recent development. The melodic line shows a clear attempt to break free from literal folk-music. The many folk-tunes scattered through the work are not, in fact, authentic, but the products of Bartók's imagination—independent creations. In this work, we may also note the first appearance of what will be one of his constant preoccupations henceforth: to group together against a classical background the greatest possible number of distinct themes and to extend them along sustained and multiple melodic lines. Bartók became an innovator precisely because he failed in this attempt. In short, his genius for melody was so prodigal that, to begin with, he was only able approximately to fit his inventions into the moulds he had chosen. Then, as this richness of melodic invention continually increased, by about 1926 he was obliged to shatter the old moulds and, by enlarging or combining some of their separate elements, to create fresh ones.

BARTÓK AND IMPRESSIONISM

BUT a danger lurked in the sheer profusion of melodic material. We all know compositions in which eleven or twelve different themes—each one, perhaps, a marvel in itself—are superimposed, whose total effect in the concert hall is one of wilful chaos. Bartók was saved from what the Latins, with justifiable disdain, refer to as the "Central European style" by the harmonies of Debussy—by what, in short, we call "Impressionism".

But "impressionism" has been so much discussed that the ideas which originally animated it have become vague and woolly. Therefore, we must attempt to redefine them, especially if we are to understand the role they played in Bartók's development. And if, in what follows, I appear to be contrasting impressionism with classicism, that is solely for the sake of clarity. It is obvious that the former derived largely from the latter, through the late works of Beethoven, through Schubert, Schumann, and Chopin. For these masters, by an increasingly subtle use of the enharmonic and the elliptical cadence, accustomed the ear to ever finer nuances, and overthrew the old rules of harmonic progression.

After the Middle Ages, the spirit of invention in music exercised itself on three elements: rhythm, melody and harmony. Now, melody can be compared to line, and harmony to volume; and lines and volumes, in music as in painting, are linked by relationships of movement, which we call rhythm. A composer, in creating a new work, may take for his starting point either a melody, or a series of harmonies which in themselves will suggest the melodic lines of which, to begin with, he is only half aware.

Having postulated this, we can go a step further, and say that the classical musician concentrates in the first place on the melody, always bearing in mind the harmonic rules of tonality, while the impressionist begins with harmonies and their progressions, while bearing in mind the empirical laws of modality. When the classical musician has organized his theme in half-periods, periods, and phrases, the harmonies which are to sustain the resulting melodic line will always, apart from a few superficial variations, be foreseeable to anyone with any knowledge of the standard text-books on composition. But when the same person is confronted with a melodic line from Mussorgsky or Debussy, the number of unforeseeable harmonies becomes considerable, and the variations, instead of being superficial, are often fundamental. And in fact the impressionist musician seeks arrangements and progressions of chords which, while they are admittedly based on harmonic experience, nevertheless escape *a priori* from the rigid scholastic convention of the major-minor and the cycle of fifths.

To sum up: the classical style arises from an intellectual architecture; memory and "tonality" are its tools. The impressionist style, on the other hand, arises from an architecture of sensations; intuition and modality are its logic, and taste its only law.

*　　　*　　　*

F

Where did impressionism stand in the year
Bartók was born—in 1881?

In France, the cradle of this style, many elements
had been brought together which Debussy was to
use. The Benedictines, Dom Pothier and Dom
Guéranger, had restored the Gregorian chant, with
its rhythmic liberty and original modality. Mediaeval airs and *motifs* had been introduced into
operas as popular as those of Léo Delibes. Technical improvements in the manufacture of pianos
had brought into the range of hearing hitherto
purely theoretical harmonies, and thus made variations of colour possible in a single sound. Out of
all these elements, Debussy was to constitute, by a
rapid synthesis, the matter of musical impressionism,
after having grasped the uninhibited methods of
Mussorgsky and applied them to Mediterranean
themes.

In 1884, Debussy wrote *L'Enfant Prodigue*, in
1893, *Le Prélude à l'Après-Midi d'un Faune*, in 1902,
Pelléas, and in 1905, *La Mer*. This extraordinary
composition marked the highest, purest and most
classic peak of the impressionist movement—and
therefore, the point also at which it was nearest
to falling into decadence. The idiom of the great
French master became hard and set in the hands
of his imitators: the school of Debussy killed Debussy. The only fresh path seemed to lie through
Stravinsky and atonalism. It fell to Bartók the
Magyar—together with Ravel the Basque, Milhaud
the Jew, and Manuel de Falla the Andalusian—

to save impressionism by transplanting it to soil of a
very different origin from Debussy's. What miracles
can be wrought by a change of climate! . . .

*   *   *

There are several reasons why impressionism
awoke such a deep response in Bartók.

In the early years of the century, the Debussy
idiom was rolling like a great wave across Europe,
with its rising and falling progressions of major
sevenths and ninths and the crystalline clash of
seconds and fifths.   No country escaped this impressionist "pollenization", already foreshadowed
in poetry, literature and painting, although, under
northern skies, it is true, the new flower bloomed
only for a few short seasons.   A Cyril Scott or a
Niemann, for example, had no followers.

But in Hungary, which has always been and
remains still in close musical and spiritual contact
with France, the new movement was bound to have
a profound influence.   Quite apart from the
historical contacts between the two cultures, there
was also the fact that impressionism, with its
central emphasis on modality, was particularly
well suited to become acclimatised in a country
where folk-music had remained so much alive.
Impressionism was to restore to Hungarian music,
in all their perennial vigour, the harmonies of
fourths and fifths, which lay at the root of her folk-

music and echoed the ancient defective scales of the East, imported into Europe in the tenth century by the Magyar horsemen of King Arpád. And Bartók himself was all the more responsive to Debussy's message for being born of country folk, and brought up among national songs and dances. The folk song was indeed the song of his essential being.

Thus, when Bartók wanted to use the ancient popular cantilena of mediaeval times, it was inevitable that he should invoke the spirit of impressionism. Faced with a melodic line so oscillating that no formula of classical tonal harmony was adapted to it, he found himself instinctively compelled to invent and create for it an adequate harmony. By doing so, he was bound to adopt Debussy's method, and to apply it subsequently to his own free compositions.

The words of Hungarian folk-songs contributed almost as much as their modal music to initiating Bartók into that "aesthetic of atmosphere" which is the true aesthetic of impressionism. Allusion, presentiment, evasion and symbol—all the mediums used by folk poetry had helped to show him the value of what is left unexpressed. Besides, the widely varied forms of Magyar poetry had given him a sense of architectural diversity. Through these influences, he was to outstrip all other modern composers in the transformations and complexities he introduced into traditional musical forms.

HUNGARIAN POPULAR POETRY

HUNGARIAN folk poetry does not consist merely of regular stanzaic constructions, made of successions of couplets or quatrains, sometimes separated by refrains, like the ballad in France and many other European countries. It abounds also in pieces in free forms, in lines linked together without rhyme or repetition, the metres varying in the course of a single poem—many Hungarian ballads are of this sort. The most ancient of these songs have only a few words, the few needed to express the mood of a tribe trudging across monotonous deserts or prairies in nomadic times. Such songs are interminably repetitious and were spoken rhapsodies before they became sung rhapsodies.

Their subjects are innumerable, as innumerable as the personal and collective hardships and pleasures of a warrior people that had become a pastoral people, and which an inexorable fate had placed at the crossroads of European tragedy. Eastern by race and western by vocation, the victim of two worlds which confronted each other across his territory, the Magyar shepherd had to be continually moving his flocks. That is why, more than of love or the joys of good living, Magyar poetry sings so often of the crusades and of the homesickness of the labourer leaving his hopes, his lands, his plough, to "go off to the wars", to swell the ranks of diehard infantry or of those famous squadrons of Hungarian cavalry who were so often to save Christianity after having, in more distant days, so often terrorized it.

The most surprising trait of Hungarian folk poetry (from the point of view of the rest of Europe, where folk poetry generally uses a clear, rational, even rather trite vocabulary) is its symbolic style and its technique of allusiveness in the use of images. This even recalls the methods of the French Symbolist movement in poetry, which was, of course, one of the sources of Impressionism in music. Obviously the techniques of Mallarmé and of an anonymous singer who says:

> My pretty lace collar from Vienna is torn,
> My tanned handsome lover has just gone away,

cannot be compared in detail; yet from the Magyar folk-song there does emerge a sense of troubled richness, familiar to Mallarmé's readers. And some techniques are the same: the presentation of an image which gives it the air of being the principal object of attention (the pretty lace collar, the brown good looks of the lover) and then the breaking-through of the true reality, of the motivating idea ("My . . . lover . . . has just gone away"). There is the same sense of gripping concision, of much in little; the couplet we have just quoted, for instance, enables us to reconstitute the whole emotional violence of a scene of parting.

This technique of allusion, common to French poets of the late nineteenth century and to the Magyar bards, sometimes obviously displays its Far Eastern origins:

> *October*
> The rain falls
> On the handles
> Of the plough.

This working-chanty, with an ample and un-wearyingly repeated melody, I have deliberately printed in three short lines and called "October" to underline its close relationship with the Japanese haiku which, as we know, has brought to an almost unequalled point of perfection the art of evocation in a few syllables. And the haiku was very much the fashion among the musicians who derived from Debussy.

The archetypal comparisons of a more traditional symbolism, which have become dull and common-place to the civilized, retain their flavour in the Magyar countryside; the folk poets do not hesitate to compare a woman to the earth, to a cornfield, giving her also the eternal attributes of Cybele:

> Corn, corn, what a fine field of corn!
> In the middle two lovely cornflowers!
> Who will look after them when we have to march,
> To march off with the regiment . . . ?

"Two cornflowers" . . . the eyes of the beloved,

whose pupils look pale against the abundant gold
("corn, corn . . .") of her hair.

The word "fire" also retains its traditional
archetypal sense of "the passion of love" but here
again the Magyar fashion of provoking associations
of ideas, starting with this image, recalls the French
symbolists:

> The cottage is burning
> The reeds are breaking
> Press to your heart
> That lovely dark girl.

Or again:

> At Kaposvár the candle burns,
> It is a lad who's lighting it,
> Now snuffing it, now lighting it,
> And filling my wounded heart with despair.

Even when the feeling is humorous or there is a
double entendre the technique remains the same:

> The belfry is very high in the sky
> And my lamb has no meadow,
> My lamb needs a good meadow
> And I a nice girl.

This rather obscure text is clarified by the following
couplet:

> Without a belfry what's a town worth,
> Without a lover what's a girl worth?

But the mood of this folk poetry is in general poignantly sad. The conscript leaving for the Army speaks of his desolate future:

Down there a gilded carriage comes,
And Mister Counsellor sits inside!
Oh, Counsellor, put down your pen,
Don't write me down among the young recruits . . .
My little angel, I must leave you then.

There flies a white turtle-dove,
Under its wing it carries a sad letter,
No one can read the writing here,
It's not even addressed in the Magyar tongue . . .
My little angel, I must leave you then.

Down there's a great forest,
Two tender branches grew there,
Each branch is withered up,
No bird puts its foot there . . .
My little angel, sad news for you!

The poet has premonitions of his death, which regimental headquarters will announce in German.

Some of these poems show a most cunning skill in composition—the way their images and ideas are linked fascinates and astonishes the professional poet.

At the door of the mayor of Gyarak
Down in the mud my hat has fallen!
O, my lover, pick up my hat!
How I regret my lovely liberty!

And in the mayor of Gyarak's courtyard
The acacia flower has shed its petals,
How many mothers would pick them all up
If only their sons could not be soldiers!

And in the mayor of Gyarak's garden
The bursting cherry has fallen down,
It is as red as spurting blood:
I die for my dear dove.

"Down in the mud my hat has fallen" is a way of saying that the speaker has changed his civilian headdress for a military shako. The point about the acacia flowers in the second stanza is that their petals are so small and light that, once they have fallen, it is impossible to pick them all up. . . .

A peasant by race, passionate by nature, but discreet in his words and gestures, Bartók cherished this allusive art with its intimate undertones. But if he received such technical lessons from Hungarian folk poetry, all the more was he confirmed in a state of mind and dedicated to receive a message whose emotional ends were attained by similar means: that of Debussy.

We can say even more than that: the subtlety of impressionist music is not intelligible except by the light of such symbolism. And one more general point may be made: impressionist music has always easily acclimatized itself in all countries where popular or folk-poetry is symbolist. In Japan, to take a striking example, the Western music that has been most widely and, from a commercial point of view, most successfully diffused is that, in the first instance, of Debussy and later that of the other modern masters who contain, for the Japanese ear, the greatest number of technical elements deriving from impressionism. In discovering French impressionism, Bartók also renewed contact with the Oriental sensibility of his ancestors.

BARTÓK'S OWN TESTIMONY

BARTÓK freely acknowledged, on numerous occasions, the determining role which Debussy had played in shaping his own personality: in his autobiography, in the obituary tribute he wrote on the French composer's death in 1918, and in his recorded words to numbers of irrefutable witnesses. I, too, heard the same tributes from his own lips.

I had the good fortune to meet Bartók for the first time in the spring of 1939. Our interview took place in a comfortable hotel in the Rue Boissy d'Anglas; and from the outset, I was forcibly impressed by Bartók's distinction and quiet elegance. He was of medium height, with a long lean face looking unnaturally youthful under his white hair and lit by a blue, sad, piercing glance. As he sat there, a slight figure in the hollow of a vast leather armchair, he gave an impression of melancholy tranquillity allied to unrelenting tension, as of a bow drawn taut; while behind the exquisite courtesy of his manner, one sensed a great reserve and modesty.

"Kodály and I wanted to make a synthesis of East and West," he told me. "Because of our race, and because of the geographical position of our country, which is at once the extreme point of the East and the defensive bastion of the West, we felt this was a task we were well fitted to undertake. But it was your Debussy, whose music had just begun to reach us, who showed us the path we must follow. And that, in itself, was a curious phenomenon when one recalls that at that time, so many French musicians were still held in thrall by the prestige of Wagner. . . ."

He paused, and then went on:

"Debussy's great service to music was to reawaken among all musicians an awareness of harmony and its possibilities. In that, he was just as important as Beethoven, who revealed to us the meaning of progressive form, and as Bach, who showed us the transcendent significance of counterpoint. . . ."

He paused to light a cigarette, and gazed before him with an abstracted air for several moments.

"Now, what I am always asking myself," he said, "is this: is it possible to make a synthesis of these three great masters, a living synthesis that will be valid for our own time? . . ."

THE SEARCH FOR A SYNTHESIS

FROM all that has been said, we can now see the problem with which Bartók was faced. Coming from non-European ancestry, and having his roots in the collective unconscious of an Oriental race, and yet having been trained in that most irrefutable of Western techniques, the European classical tradition, Bartók set himself the task of reconciling these contraries. The dualism lay deep in his own nature, and it was from this conflict between opposed poles that Bartók's whole drama arose. From 1935 on, furthermore, Bartók was to render that problem explicit, not by the facile abstraction of theoretical writings, but by actual compositions which were only brought into being with immense difficulty.

It was an obscure struggle, and we cannot but admire the energy and lucidity with which he pursued it for more than twenty-five years. Now, however, looking back over the whole range of the composer's works, we can see perhaps more clearly than Bartók himself could at the time what it really involved. He was attempting to synthesize the modal and the tonal, impressionism and German classicism. What Bartók really tried to do, in other words, was to break down the representative framework of German descriptive music, which tended to attach itself to the pole of movement, by integrating in it the tendency of Mediterranean descriptive music to attach itself to the psychological pole. It was an attempt to harmonize Franz Liszt's years of pilgrimage with the twenty-four *Préludes* of Claude de France—to marry the demon of Strauss to the muse of Claude Debussy.

CONTRAPUNTAL EXPERIMENTS AND DISCOVERIES

AN event which occurred in 1907 crowned Bartók's career as a pianist, and also secured for him an official position. His old master, Thomán, resigned, and Bartók succeeded him in charge of the advanced piano class at the Budapest Academy. The future seemed to be smiling on him, and he plunged joyfully into work. Soon he had completed his *Two Portraits* for orchestra, his first serious attempt to use purely contrapuntal material. This composition was also a tribute to friendship, for one of the people who had inspired it was Emma Gruber, a young woman who had been Bartók's pupil and who had just married his friend Zoltán Kodály. In the first section, the superimposed lines of the sharply outlined andante move towards fulfilment in the turbulence of the finale in the second section. Looking back now, the work can be seen to have certain weaknesses—in particular, some of the cadential pauses lack the feeling of inevitability. But we can also see that the andante of the *Portraits* was the forerunner of the extraordinary andante of the *Music for Strings, Percussion and Celesta*, and that the waltz of the second section foreshadowed the demoniac three-four finale of the *Symphonic Suite* taken from *The Wonderful Mandarin*.

In *Two Portraits*, Bartók had broken through his former technical limits with a work for orchestra. In 1908, with the *Fourteen Bagatelles*, it was through the medium of the piano that he demonstrated once more the extraordinary range of his intelligence and his intuition. Indeed Arnold Schönberg, in his *Treatise on Harmony*, even cited one of Bartók's discoveries in this work—a rare honour, since he was the only foreign musician quoted. And Bartók himself, writing to the learned musicologist Edwin von der Nüll, described several of the *Bagatelles* (numbers 1, 8, 9, 11 and 13) as "experiments". What he was trying to do here was to draw the ultimate consequences from both harmony and counterpoint as he then understood them, to reach a new equilibrium by a combination of the laws fixing the limits of each. Number 1 is a study in polymelodism; 8 is a study in the harmony of the major seventh; 9, a quest for pure melodic design (left and right hands play a strongly defined melody in unison); 11, an exercise on the chord of the thirteenth on the dominant; 13, an exercise in the harmonic integration of pedal notes.

Fourteen Bagatelles are of central significance in Bartók's work, marking the end of one period and the beginning of another. Later, when mingled with the impressionist ambience and the implicit harmony of the folk-song, they were indeed to form the climate in which many of Bartók's subsequent ideas developed: they were, in other words, the soil from which sprang the two *Sonatas for Violin and Piano* (1921 and 1922), the *Mikrokosmos*, for piano (1926 to 1937), and the *Contrasts*, for violin, clarinet and piano (1938).

The new style aroused much opposition. As Kodály wrote in the *Revue Musicale* in March, 1921: "... people objected to its lack of melody, its superabundance of dissonances, its lack of construction, its disorder and incoherence which made it 'incomprehensible'. Finally, they began to say it was not truly Hungarian in character. But do we not hear the same complaints whenever anything genuinely new in art appears? ... All the dilettantes clamour for—melody! Certainly, one no longer finds in these works the good old clichés of Hungarian music, nor that Italo-German melody which for centuries has been regarded as the only valid article of its kind. And yet, if we try to express the essence of Bartók's new style, we are bound to call it a renaissance of both melody and rhythm."

The *Bagatelles* were indeed greeted with sarcasm, anger, and furious disputes for Bartók, they heralded a difficult and turbulent period.

BARTÓK'S DUALISM

THE same year, 1908, saw the birth of a work no less significant than the *Bagatelles* as a pointer to Bartók's later development. This was the *First String Quartet* in A (Opus 7). This work represents the first instance of Bartók's urge to transcend a double loyalty—first, to harmony, the pianist's initial and instinctive choice, and secondly, to a linear architecture, the more conscious choice of the composer's intelligence. Throughout his creative life, Bartók was to struggle for a new equilibrium between vertical and horizontal forces. The *Fifth Quartet*, the *Music for String Orchestra and Celesta* and the *Violin Concerto* attained such an equilibrium, but they were not to be written until many years later. Meanwhile Bartók came under the influence of these two forces alternately. In one work he would start with harmonic groupings, in the next he would concentrate on contrapuntal complexities; and so it went on. In between bouts of wrestling with these contradictory tendencies, he still went on collecting and harmonizing folk songs.

The *First Quartet* is not only a work of great beauty, it is also essential to an understanding of the renewed aesthetic meaning which Bartók was to give to the quartet form. At many points in it we are reminded of Beethoven's last quartets, particularly the fourteenth: the fugue-like style of the first movement, the fugue which closes the last, the syncopated rhythm of the first section—all these seem to refer back to that great model in C.

One final point is worth noting: in the slow fugue which opens this work Bartók employs the twelve notes of the chromatic scale between the first subject and counter-statement. It was the first time he had confronted that problem of total chromaticism and of the twelve-tone aesthetic about which so much ink is spilt to-day.

G

PIANO COMPOSITIONS, 1908–9

FOR Bartók 1908 was a feverishly active year. In this period he turned to writing for the piano, producing a series of works with the teacher's purpose in mind: these comprise *Ten Easy Pieces* and *For Children* (eighty-five short pieces of gradually increasing difficulty, completed in 1909), *Two Elegies*, and finally *Three Burlesques*. In these works, apart from the elegies—which Bartók himself wittily describes as "a return to the old romantic afflatus"—the atmosphere is one of good humour, joviality, the robust moral health of a man ready for a joke, and avowing it in such indications of tempo as "a little drunken" at the beginning of the *Second Burlesque*. But by the use of distortions necessary to the humorous purpose of the *Burlesques*, and the decorative variations of folk motifs in *For Children*, Bartók put into practice his discoveries in harmony and rhythm—an acid harmony here, a slack and easy rhythm there—and thus, under cover of laughter and deliberate charm—new uses of sound infiltrated into the sensibility of his hearers and in the long run modified it.

In 1909 Bartók once more succumbed to the attractions of folk-music, which provided most of the ideas for his *Two Rumanian Dances* for piano, completed in early 1910. This return to the "sacred wood" of the Folk-Muse also prepared a fresh surprise—that of the *Four Funeral Chants*.

These four piano pieces are profoundly moving, with their rich harmonies, their opaline luminosity, and their surprising use of the impressionist palette. One thinks of them at times as preludes that Debussy forgot to add to his two famous collections; but Bartók cannot have owed anything to these, since Debussy's first twelve preludes were not published in Paris until 1910, some months after the completion of the *Funeral Chants*. The first of the four is, indeed, too chromatic to be attributed to Debussy, but the second curiously foreshadows his *Canope Endormie*, despite its use—adventurous for the period —of the major-minor. The fact that Debussy and Bartók should have developed in such a parallel fashion lends a singular force to the logic of the impressionist theory. *Four Funeral Chants*, in addition, proves once more that the instrument on which a composer plays helps to crystallize his inspiration: for nobody but a virtuoso of the piano would have been able to extract from the keyboard the resounding fullness of *Funeral Chant* No. 3, or to attain the dramatic effect of the crescendo in No. 4, achieved by the piling up of massed harmonies.

This work, however, also has a psychological importance. Here Bartók deliberately reveals the darker side of his temperament, and in doing so gives retrospective authenticity to his earlier romantic outbursts, which we might otherwise suspect of being "literary", or of being assiduously modelled on Liszt, Wagner and Strauss. Now we are able to understand why, throughout his life, Bartók was to express himself lyrically and why he was so often to be tempted by total chromaticism, the familiar instrument of modern expressionism.

EARLY BATTLES

BARTÓK'S achievements in the use of impressionist techniques were not always so successful as *Four Funeral Chants*. Among those which may be mentioned are the *Sketches* for piano, completed in 1910. In these, beneath broad melodic lines, Bartók simultaneously and deliberately blended ecclesiastical and tonal modes, merging both into a mobile harmonic mass. Similar problems of synthesis crop up once more in the *Two Images* for orchestra, which followed. Here, however, the solutions proposed are more convincing, because the "literary" atmosphere embodied in the titles *Flowering* and *Village Festival* kept Bartók down to earth, as it were, while the second piece is agreeably enhanced by its echoes of actual folk-music.

From the orchestral point of view, *Two Images* is a complete success: the economy of tonal colours, the purity and refinement of the orchestration, the variation of densities, the skilful management of perspectives, all indicate a new grasp of the orchestra as an instrument, and foreshadow the rich palette that was to cause Bartók often to be compared with Stravinsky. At the same time, Bartók, with his sturdy Magyar temperament, was able to elude the enticements of harmony for its own sake unaided by firm melodic outlines.

The dynamic qualities of his race and temperament are well illustrated by another work—the famous *Allegro Barbaro* for piano, written and finished in a single burst at the end of 1910 and the beginning of 1911. This is a work packed with explosive elements which are detonated by contact with an elemental rhythm—Bartók's own fundamental rhythm. Here, for the first time, he unleashed that rhythm with a sort of fury that has all the air of a challenge provoked by the incomprehension of some of his opponents. He seems to be trying to shock people—and indeed he succeeded! Once more there was an outcry against him.

Time has justified the composer, and to-day we can see how truly effective are his almost mathematical use of the ternary form and the F-sharp tonality. This brilliant work has now become a favourite concert encore.

But at that period, *Allegro Barbaro* goaded the conservatives to full fury; in fact, almost all the professional composers—except, of course, Ernst Dohnányi and Kodály—rose up in arms against it. Kodály himself has told us, in the article quoted earlier, how ". . . their opposition verged on persecution. People spoke of a great talent on the wrong path, 'lost down a blind alley', of 'morbid tendencies'—in short, all the phrases to be expected of dismayed Philistines and the slaves of convention. Some even began to regard Bartók as insane!"

But Bartók was not a man to be intimidated. On the contrary, he went over to the attack. That same year, together with Kodály, he organized a chamber music society, and there was even talk of putting on orchestral concerts later. But the inevitable happened: by the second concert, the society's funds were exhausted. The "slaves of convention" were jubilant; the new French and Hungarian music seemed to be safely buried, and with it, the ancient unknown music of the Hungarian past!

BLUEBEARD'S CASTLE, 1911

GIVEN the unpopularity of Bartók with conventional minds, we can imagine what thoughts passed through the heads of the Commission of Fine Arts, assembled in Budapest in 1911 to award a prize to the best Hungarian lyrical work of the year, when they found themselves faced with the one-act opera, *Bluebeard's Castle*, composed by Bartók on a libretto by Béla Balázs. Such juries are always more the servants of prudence than of virtue; this one, in addition, was besotted with the German tradition . . . and with rage; the work was rejected with cries of, "Unplayable!". "It's unplayable"—the phrase is a kind of repeated chorus in the history of music, whenever a creator appears who is a little more skilful and cunning than his brothers. Posterity always gives the creators their revenge. Bartók had not to wait long. In 1918 *Bluebeard's Castle* was put on at the National Opera in Budapest and aroused great enthusiasm. . . .

Kodály explains the reason for its triumph: ". . . *Bluebeard's Castle* is for us what *Pelléas* is for France. If we can say that, in spite of the glorious past of the French lyrical theatre, a type of musical declamation that suited the genius of the language did not exist before Debussy, how much truer such a statement is in our own case in relation to Bartók. From the time of the first operas written in the Hungarian language (around 1833), the number of original works has always been restricted and our repertory encumbered with foreign works in detestable translations which were an insult to our tongue. Even the authors of original Hungarian operas could not free themselves from this 'opera dialect'. By respecting in his recitatives the natural music of our language and, in the more stylized parts of his opera, the tone of Hungarian folk music, Bartók opened a new road. But at the same time he created a work of irresistible suggestive power. The seven doors of Bluebeard's castle, opening one by one, give rise to musical images that are not externally 'descriptive' but express the most intimate feeling. Only impenitent pedants can go on asking themselves whether this is 'really' an opera or not. What does it matter? Call it a 'scenic symphony' or a 'drama accompanied by a symphony', what matters is that it is impossible to separate the music and the drama, and that here we have a masterpiece, a musical fountain that

erupts for sixty minutes of compressed tragedy and
leaves us only with one desire: the desire to hear it
again . . .".[1]

Béla Balázs had his subject suggested to him by
Ariane et Barbe-Bleue, ou la Délivrance Inutile, a
libretto written by Maurice Maeterlinck for the
French musician, Paul Dukas. Had the Hungarian
poet seen this lyrical drama on its first presentation
at the Opéra-Comique in Paris in 1907? It is a
point which should be cleared up, whatever the
answer may be, for the theme, as treated by both
librettists, owes nothing to Perrault's fairy-tale.
The way in which Balázs handles the idea he derives
from Maeterlinck is very original, and the moral he
draws from this grim story is more weighty, less
ornamental, than that drawn by the Belgian
dramatist.

Before the orchestra plays its overture or the
curtain goes up, a bard recites a ballad with a
mysterious significance: "They pass judgment on
you and on me, ladies and gentlemen," he says,
"these old stories . . . we are all guilty or all inno-
cent."

We have been warned; we are going to enter into
the region of symbolism; behind the veil of
appearances, a fundamental truth will lie hidden.

The curtain rises; the scene represents the main
hall of the Duke's castle; it is damp and dark, but
we can distinguish seven doors with heavy bolts.
Bluebeard and Judith enter; happiness is still

[1] Kodály, *op. cit.*

possible, it is their wedding night, and it is Bluebeard who has been ravished by the determination of Judith.

BLUEBEARD: Why have you followed me, Judith?

JUDITH: To dry up the waters that sweat through these walls, to dry them from my lips . . . to dissipate the overwhelming sombreness . . . to make joy enter . . . the happy wind, the gay light . . . (*suddenly she sees the doors*) . . . seven great sinister doors . . . sinister closed doors . . . give me, give me the keys, quickly!

Bluebeard gives her a key, saying, "Blessed be thy hand, Judith!" The door springs open at once; a fierce red light spreads everywhere; it is the light of the torture chamber.

JUDITH: . . . chains, scourges, pincers, a wheel . . . all the stone walls bleed, there is blood everywhere . . . give me the other keys. . . .

BLUEBEARD: Why do you force me? Already my walls are trembling. Open if you will, or close, but take care, have a care for yourself, have a care for me, take care, Judith!

Obstinately the young woman unbars and unlocks the second door.

JUDITH: Swords, lances, bows and arrows, a hundred horrid engines of war!

BLUEBEARD: It is my store of weapons, Judith!

JUDITH: All bloody! . . . give me the keys of the other doors . . . already the light is creeping in, the light begins to shine . . . it is out of love that I have come, open quickly the seven doors.

BLUEBEARD: Take the keys of three more . . . open if you will, but do not question me. . . .

The third bolt yields.

JUDITH: What wealth! A huge treasure! How much gold, how many precious stones, diamonds, rubies, pearls—and glittering crowns!

BLUEBEARD: It is my treasure!

JUDITH: Blood is flowing among the ornaments . . . there is blood on the lovely crown.

BLUEBEARD: Open the fourth door to the light! Quick, quick!

JUDITH: Oh what a lovely garden! How delightful! So many flowers under these dark walls . . . how lovely the great white lilies are! Delicious perfumes, brilliant roses, ranunculus, red lilies of the valley . . . but horror still, everywhere blood is flowing . . . blood is watering the earth. . . .

BLUEBEARD: Ask no questions . . . open the fifth door.

The door conceals a huge landscape, a fertile countryside.

JUDITH: Great and wide are your domains . . . but that red cloud is bleeding . . . whence comes that red cloud? Let us open the two last doors.

BLUEBEARD: Let us leave these two doors shut, look, my arms are waiting for you . . . come, I love you.

JUDITH: Open, open, quickly!

BLUEBEARD: Do not ask it for mercy, Judith, Judith!

But Judith is in the grip of fate; she opens the

sixth door; under the vaults of a cellar something shines feebly.

JUDITH: White waters, sad waters, motionless, white waters! Whence come these funereal waters?

BLUEBEARD: Tears, Judith, tears, tears.

JUDITH: Sleeping waters, grieving waters. . . .

From this moment the drama plunges much more deeply into the indefinite sources of the psyche.

JUDITH: Tell me quickly . . . have you loved other women?

BLUEBEARD: You bring me joy, light. Love me, do not ask questions. . . .

JUDITH: Were they more beautiful, did you love them better—more tenderly? Answer me, Bluebeard . . . open the seventh door, for I have guessed, Bluebeard, what that door hides. All the blood sullying your weapons, the blood on the crown, the roots that bleed, the bleeding, sinister sky . . . I have understood whence comes the sad lake of tears. There are your wives, murdered . . . open quickly, so that I may know, open the last door.

BLUEBEARD: So be it . . . so be it . . . take the last key. All my wives are there. Look, there are my wives, those whom I loved before you.

Three women come out and move towards Bluebeard who falls on his knees.

BLUEBEARD: Lovely, lovely beloved ones, you are not forgotten. You have brought me riches, you made my roses grow, you extended my splendid domains. All that is here is yours.

JUDITH: How lovely they are, how rich! I am poor
and humble.

BLUEBEARD: In the dawn, the first came to me,
adorned with roses . . . the second stood shining
in the burning light of noon . . . the third at
twilight approached me in the calm shades . . .
in the night I found thee, Judith, in the night
sown with stars!

JUDITH: For mercy's sake, be silent, be silent . . .
I am still here!

On the threshold of the third door, Bluebeard
picks up a cloak, a crown and jewels, and adorns
Judith with them.

JUDITH: O, have pity! Not that crown. Have pity,
not this adornment!

BLUEBEARD: Now nothing but the darkness,
nothing but the darkness for ever . . .

Then Judith followed by the three other women
enters into the seventh door.

What can the significance of this story be? In
man's interior world, perhaps, there are secrets
locked away; each one of us contains the best and the
worst, the best stained by the worst, by our material
condition; the secrets are ranged all round us sealed
and mute, as mute as the seven doors of Bluebeard's
castle. Only the shining intoxication of fresh love
can sometimes dissipate this dark threat; but let the
new woman in a man's life be discreet; the hidden
places of the masculine self are forbidden to her
and above all those where, richly adorned by
kindly memory, past loves live. However total a

passion may be, it will not survive their exhuma-
tion.

One could also consider Béla Balázs's text from the
obvious angle of its obsession with cruelty, or from
the point of view of psychoanalysis. But there is
little point in such a commentary, since Bartók's
musical transformation of the theme goes far more
deep than the most subtle exegesis. Nevertheless,
according to what a Hungarian friend tells me,
Bartók seems to have favoured an interpretation of
the poem rather similar to that which I have just
given.

The opera certainly produces a striking effect on
its hearers. We are, as it were, invaded by a flux of
sometimes contradictory images, operative at every
level of our being, through the inflexible consistency
of the music, the sustained drama, the tenacity with
which the work as a whole leads our imagination
towards every possible source of the symbolism, and
the irresistible attraction of the orchestral accompaniment which gives the mood of the whole piece
volume and resonance.

The musical techniques employed are astonishing:
their synchronization shows a mastery which is
certainly not the product of intelligence and will
alone: we are forced to perceive the part played by
intuition and a close relationship with the deep,
instinctive sources of life—both of which are the
prerogatives of genius. It was through these gifts
that the thirty-year old musician was able to
achieve his purposes.

We should also emphasize the absence throughout the work of post-romantic expressionism, an absence all the more striking in a musician formed by Wagner and Strauss. Is it rash to see in this absence the result of a happy understanding of the impressionist spirit? I think not, for the orchestration and style of this work seem to me to show some affinities with those of Claude de France. Nevertheless, *Bluebeard's Castle* owes less to the French master than has been said. Leos Janácek certainly had a share in its conception and in its harmony. This was very natural, since *Jenufa*, one of the Czech composer's masterpieces, which had its triumphant first performance in Brno in 1904, had in succeeding years been several times performed in the opera houses and concert halls of the Danube basin.

FURTHER PIANO COMPOSITIONS 1912-16

ON learning that *Bluebeard's Castle* had been rejected, Bartók wished the jury to the devil, and furiously pursued his own path. In 1912 he was once more fully occupied with collecting folk-music and in publishing *Four Popular Hungarian Songs* for male choir. Back in Budapest, he composed and had performed *Four Pieces for Orchestra*, vigorously constructed even in their lyrical sections. Their brilliance, with the unmistakable reflections of impressionism, captivated the musical élite, who were now at last won over to Bartók's side.

"Perhaps he is a madman—but what a temperament!" they began to murmur, to such good effect that Count Banffy, controller of the Opera House in Budapest, feeling that at last he had sufficient support, decided to risk annoying the sacrosanct Commission of Fine Arts by commissioning a ballet from Bartók. This courageous decision was taken in 1913. Bartók was just back from a new piece of field-work, this time not in Hungary, but in the territories round Biskra, in Algeria.

Taking fresh heart, Bartók asked his friend Béla Balázs for a new libretto. The latter suggested *The Wooden Prince*, and Bartók agreed. He was to work on this theme until 1916. During this period, however, it was never his sole task—which explains the abnormally long delay in composition for a concentrated and tenacious artist who never dissipated his energies.

In 1913 also, eighteen pieces *For Beginners at the Piano* were published. They had the same practical teaching purpose as *For Children*, for in them Bartók was clarifying his ideas on the difficult art of teaching modern music, ideas that were to find their complete expression in the pages of *Mikrokosmos*.

The originality and usefulness of Bartók's teaching work ought to be underlined at this point. If you open one of Czerny's manuals or a volume of Chopin's *Etudes*, for instance, you will notice that each chapter or study deals with a particular formula, and that the great classical works for the piano, from which such formulae are taken and for

whose execution they pave the way, often use them
in series: thirds, octaves, sixths, arpeggios, and so
on, linked together in the classical chain of development. However great the originality and the difficulty of classical piano compositions may be, they all
aim at convenience of execution and are based on
a balance between the two hands. We have musical
material in which continuity is the implicit rule—
we have, in short, what has been called "pianism".

In modern writing for the piano, on the contrary,
discontinuity is nearly always the rule. After a
seventh, one finds two or three thirds, followed by
an arpeggio, then a second or a fourth, then a change
of octave: in short, a whole assembly of contradictory, unforeseeable sections or details which are the
bane of the lazy performer. This new style of
piano composition comes from the modern pre-
ponderance of two elements: the predetermined
counterpointing of sharply defined melodic lines,
and the play of a harmony of complex chords
disposed freely on the tonal palette.

Whether we accept or reject this new style, we
must give Bartók his due for perceiving that students
must be given a special preparatory training in
interpreting the works of contemporary masters.

But 1914 had arrived, bringing war in its train.
For Bartók, the war posed a particularly agonizing
problem. Fate had placed him in the German
camp, yet his most ardent desire was to see his
beloved country defeated, so that, as the old
empires fell apart, it might regain its former

independence. He isolated himself, concentrated on his work, and composed concurrently with *The Wooden Prince* a ravishing *Sonatina for Piano* (1915), based on Rumanian folk motifs. This work is, however, a "suite" rather than a sonatina, while the *Piano Suite* of 1916 is—by a charming and no doubt involuntary paradox—much more a sonata than a suite!

The folk music of Rumania, with its picturesque rhythms and lyricism, gave Bartók the idea, in this same year, 1915, of transcribing and adapting for piano the Christmas songs of the neighbouring country. He collected them under the title *Colindas*. And as he had found an orchestral point of balance in the *Two Images*, so he now found a pianistic point of balance in the three works just cited.

BARTÓK'S MELODIES

IN his youthful period, wishing to make himself immediately intelligible to his audience, Bartók chose for the themes of his compositions those that came direct from folk symbolism—as in *Bluebeard's Castle* and the *Cantata Profana*—or which, at least in their mood, suggested the folk-song and ballad. Such were the poems of Ady (1877-1919), for which he wrote five settings.

It seems to me that Bartók may well have chosen these particular poems—deriving from the metrical traditions of anonymous bards—much more as

H

pretexts for an intimate revelation of self than merely
as motives for composition. During that terrible
year of 1916, Bartók may well have wished both to
reaffirm his Hungarian attachments, in the midst of
the catastrophe unleashed by Germany, and to
reveal to us hitherto unsuspected aspects of his
personality.

Furthermore, Ady has been recognized as a
great national poet (he has been called the
Hungarian Baudelaire), and his poems faithfully
reflect the Magyar psychology. Therefore I have
felt it necessary to include a translation of those
poems which Bartók chose for his melodies:

Autumn Tears

Autumn days, autumn days,
Weary! How at the young girls
Can I still smile? . . .

Autumn nights, autumn nights,
Weary! How, without tears,
Still gaze at the stars? . . .

Autumn nights, autumn days,
Ah! The sweet fervour
Of my tears. . . .

Rumour of Autumn

So what is that vague noise?
In the folds of the autumn mist
someone is sighing in the depth of the night.

Someone is getting drunk on the world's grief
and someone is breaking the dead branches.

It is an ancestor! . . .
In the old days his sky was never bright with stars
and to-day, what the Universe may be worth
he wanders on his way, seeking.

My Bed Calls Me

Here I am, o bed.
O bed, last year
how different you were,
different, full of hope,
full of hope and strength,
strength and tenderness,
tenderness and joy. . . .
And joy now?
Now a black coffin,
coffin day after day,
coffin you grip me close,
you grip me at evening,
at evening it's anguish,
it's anguish on waking,
waking to anguish. . . .

I awake and look round,
I look round and I see,
I see and reflect,
reflect and grasp,
grasp with hesitation,
I hesitate and prop myself,

I prop myself and straighten up,
I straighten up and make ready,
I strain myself and fall back!
Shame of my heart, o bed,
o bed, o black coffin,
black coffin, you take me,
you take me . . . here I am.

Alone With the Sea

Night . . . the sea-front, the hotel room. . . .
She has gone and will not come back,
she has gone and will not come back.

On the sofa she's left some flowers. . . .
My arm clings to this old, old sofa. . . .
my arm clings to this old, old sofa. . . .

Like a kiss her scent stays with me. . . .
The sea! The sea is dancing! It is gay,
The sea! The sea is dancing! It is gay!

A lighthouse flings from far its golden flame. . .
Come my love, the sea sings and is leaping!
Come my love, the sea sings and is leaping!

Wild, the sea is singing its songs,
and I on the old sofa am dreaming,
and I on the old sofa am dreaming . . .

And here I had her heart . . . and she was mine.
The sea, the sea is singing me songs of the past,
the sea, the sea is singing me songs of the past.

I Cannot Go Towards You

Do you not want to be any longer the madness
I love?
   And I, I am dying!

Sing, sing, others are hoping, are looking, are
living,
   And I, I am dying!

O arms so white, you are tired of grasping me,
   And I, I am dying!

Nothing any more, lips, road, life, nothing has
meaning,
   And I, I am dying!

THE BALLET *THE WOODEN PRINCE* (1917)

PERHAPS the fact that it was composed in the dark
war years lends the ballet *The Wooden Prince* its
atmosphere of tragic irony. Certain critics have
claimed that it was not a suitable theme for a
ballet: and certainly, a sort of strident pessimism
runs through the whole work. But let the reader
judge for himself.

In a certain enchanted country, a Princess is
happily dancing. The park gate opens, and the
Prince appears. A fairy tells the royal ballerina to
retire into her castle. The Prince, charmed by this
lovely vision, wishes to follow her; but the trees of

the forest suddenly begin to dance in their turn,
and bar his way. The Prince is stupefied at first, but
confronts the trees boldly, and at length makes his
way through them.   But the guardian fairy is
watching, and now sets a stream to bar his path.
Discouraged, the Prince is about to admit defeat.
Then, suddenly, he has an inspiration. He makes a
wooden puppet, clothes it in his royal cloak, and
waves it before him.   The Princess has been
watching from a distance, but her lover's gestures
seem to leave her indifferent. The latter replaces
the cloak by his golden crown, and once more waves
the puppet before him. The Princess sees what is
happening, but still does not budge. Finally, the
Prince cuts off his hair and sets it on the puppet's
head; and at last, as if hypnotized, the Princess
begins to descend the steps of the castle. The fairy
touches the puppet lightly three times with her
wand, and the puppet springs to life and starts to
gesticulate. The Princess takes the puppet lovingly
into her arms, and goes off with it, without paying the
least attention to the Prince, who still tries to
pursue her.   Finally, overcome with despair, the
Prince sinks to the ground and falls asleep. . . .

     The fairy departs from the forest. Things spring
to life again, and gradually crowd round the sleeper.
Trees, streams and flowers all glorify him, decking
him out in a new crown and cloak, even in a new
head of hair.   Meanwhile, the wooden puppet,
exhausted and barely able to stand, leaves the
castle still in the embrace of the Princess.   The

latter turns away from the wretched manikin, and suddenly sees the Prince, is filled with wonderment, and invites him to follow her. But the Prince places his hand on his heart, shakes his head, and begins to move away. And now, it is the Princess's turn to pursue the object of her desire; but once again, the forest springs to life and intervenes to block her path. In despair, the young woman snatches off her crown, cuts her hair off, and sinks to the ground, weeping. The Prince reappears, and the Princess, ashamed to be seen cropped and stripped of her grandeur, tries to flee. But the Prince catches and holds her in a long embrace; and at once objects take on their old forms and resume their habitual postures while the curtain slowly falls.

This ingenious fable contains the same moral as Perrault's fairy story, *Beauty and the Beast*: man, held in thrall by appearances, does not perceive the precious nature of beings and things until a sacrificial act has been performed.

The mounting of the ballet presented enormous difficulties, both from the point of view of the music and of the choreography. They were overcome, however, thanks to the energy of the Italian conductor Egisto Tango, who was in Budapest from 1912 to 1919.

The compact orchestration and the sharp definition of the themes in *The Wooden Prince* show us another side to Bartók's temperament which we might not have suspected from the sustained lyricism of *Bluebeard's Castle*. In fact, given a subject reflecting on human behaviour, Bartók was prone to express himself with considerable acerbity; and it is this side to his nature of which we catch glimpses in the different sections of the ballet—in the dances when trees and stream prevent the mortal Prince from pursuing his Princess, and in the parodic violence of the scene when the Princess embraces the puppet. . . .

This tendency relates Bartók to Stravinsky, and explains the influence of *Petrushka* on certain passages and moods of *The Wooden Prince*. It also confers on the numerous folk-song settings and the *Five Melodies* for poems by Ady, all written while the ballet was being composed, a curious quality of compensatory psychic activity, which should not, perhaps, surprise us in a man at once tormented and driven onwards by a fundamental inner dualism.

SECOND STRING QUARTET (1915–17)

BARTÓK'S rhythmic imagination had been re-awakened by the extended choreography of *The Wooden Prince* and by the many harmonizations of folk-songs which he made during this period. These works no doubt helped to inspire the *Second String Quartet*—one might even say that it is a sort of synthesis of folk-music motifs carried into the domain of pure music. It was begun in 1915 and finished shortly after the ballet; indeed, the fate of these two works continued to be linked, since both were given their first performances in 1918.

The *Second String Quartet* is remarkable not only for the richness of its rhythmical and harmonic complexities, but also for its originality of form. It is in three parts—each, at first glance, an autonomous entity. It is only when we have heard the whole work that we are able to perceive its underlying unity. The first movement, an allegro in sonata form, prepares the mind by its polyphonic progression for the tension of the second—a startling scherzo full of breath-taking rhythmical complexities. The third movement begins with a contrapuntal grouping comparable to the first, but in andante time, which gradually broadens out until it absorbs all the given melodic outlines. Thus we have a work obeying the laws of a compact psychic cycle: preparation of tension—tension—relaxation.

RHYTHM AS AN ARCHITECTURAL FUNCTION

IN classical works, rhythm is almost always subordinated to the exigencies of melodic development. Among the few exceptions to this rule are certain *Preludes* and *Organ Fantasies* of Johann Sebastian Bach—wonderful works which, be it noted in passing, are played all too seldom. In these pieces, rhythm seems to burst the thematic framework asunder, blowing it away on the winds of an impetuous inspiration. It is as though the only

function of the notes were to convey movement
first and foremost, in a prodigious arithmetical
efflorescence. The greatness of Bartók is to have
gradually rediscovered this secret, and boldly to
have explored its unknown potentialities. He was,
indeed, sensitive to the psychic laws of rhythm to
such a degree that, when we look at some of his
finest works, we can even speak of rhythm as
providing the theme.

It is in Bartók's *Studies* for piano that the allure-
ments of rhythm for its own sake begin to make
themselves clearly felt. For here it is rhythm that
binds together the different sections, based on large
harmonic leaps sustained by rapid flights of
arpeggios. We may notice, also, the weakening of
the traditional role of the cadence and the multipli-
cation of contrapuntal suggestions. Here, Bartók is
striving towards a "more ample tonality"—to use
the excellent expression of Herr von der Null (*op. cit.*).

With this work, and the *Second String Quartet*
which preceded it, a new manner makes itself felt.
Counterpoint struggles against harmony: the horizontal complex of melody and rhythm strives to
dominate the vertical complex of harmony and
metre. And it is not only a question of the counterpoint of the melodic lines, but also that of the
harmonies and rhythms. There has been much talk
of the influences which Bartók underwent at this
period, notably those of Stravinsky and Schönberg:
but of the former, he knew only the *Sacre* and the
Rossignol in piano arrangements, and of the latter

only the two collections of piano pieces of 1909 and 1911. He knew none of their orchestral works, for the Budapest Philharmonic Society encountered quite enough difficulties in performing the works of young Hungarian composers, without complicating its task by presenting those of revolutionary foreigners.

Bartók had above all drawn what one might call the grammatical conclusions from his own wide background knowledge of contemporary music, and had projected into the musical climate of the time his special impulse as a unique master of rhythm. It was, besides, this rigorous concern for rhythm which saved him from wandering down unprofitable by-paths into which his curiosity might otherwise have led him.

THE WONDERFUL MANDARIN (1919)

THE whole of this ballet, composed in 1919 round a theme by Melchior Lengyel, manifests the supremacy of rhythm and its conceptual dominance. French musicians quickly grasped the significance of this aspect of the work when it was performed for the first time in Paris. Suzanne Demarquez has strikingly summed up their reaction in an article in the *Revue Musicale*: "He adapted for the concert hall almost the whole of the first part of the work, and turned it into a symphonic fragment in which it is not difficult to discern the three classical phases: an allegro, a slow movement—in this

case a waltz—and a finale. The unity of action,
if I may put it so, is thus preserved. So is the
unity of style, thanks to the rhythmic necessities
of the dance—necessities which Bartók imposes
with despotic rigour. Here we have the Bartók
we know—an absolute master of rhythm, which
he handles like a first-class technician, and the
master also of tone colours which he builds up
with consummate art. In *The Wonderful Mandarin*,
there is no folk-music, and little or nothing in the
way of melodic themes; but there are syncopated
rhythms, massive and extremely dissonant harmonies
repeated again and again, and a deliberate disorder
which soon gives the impression of an orgy of
sounds, among which we can distinguish the
strident peals of the brass, and then, by way of
contrast, a very distant murmuring, almost melting
away. . . . In the finale, there is nothing that one
could call a theme: at most, two notes (a descending
third, and an arpeggio) are the point of departure
for a dance which works itself into a frenzy of
noise and movement. The whole work creates an
impression of intense vitality, but vitality stretched
to its utmost limits. . . ."

This work had no better fortune on the stage than
its two predecessors—*Bluebeard's Castle* and *The
Wooden Prince*. It was claimed that the theme was not
moral enough, and the work was withdrawn. This
was a slender enough excuse, as the reader may
judge from an outline of the plot.

In a squalid hovel live three vagabonds and a

girl. The three tramps ask the girl to stop the passers-by and lure them inside, and after much hesitation she agrees. She executes a charming dance which first attracts an old, comic merchant. But soon he becomes arrogant and violent. The three vagabonds enter, rob him, and throw him out. Once more they tell the girl to dance in front of the window. A timid young man now presents himself, but as he has no money they immediately show him out. Yet a third time the girl begins her dance.

And now, in the street, a strange-looking individual can be seen approaching the dancer. The three tramps hide. The mandarin enters, and remains rooted to the spot. After a long, frozen silence the girl, with cunning gestures, begins to weave a spell around him. The mandarin rushes madly after her. (It is at this point that the concert suite adapted from the ballet ends.) The three tramps enter, fall upon the mandarin, strip him of his riches, and try to smother him with pillows, finally leaving him for dead. But the mandarin revives, totters to his feet, and continues to pursue the girl. The three tramps run him through with a rusty sword, but desire drives him on. In the end, they hang him, but his imploring eyes continue to stare at the girl. The latter, overcoming her initial terror, orders the tramps to cut him down. They obey. She makes a sign to them to go out. The mandarin, now free, leaps upon the girl, who no longer resists him. They embrace; but now the mandarin, finding his desire fulfilled, begins to lose blood from his wounds, grows weaker and weaker, and dies after a brief death struggle.

Bartók never had the pleasure of seeing his devoted friend, Egisto Tango, produce his third work for the stage. A succession of historic events prevented it, and Budapest did not see *The Wonderful Mandarin* until 1945, some weeks after the composer's death. Up to that time, Budapest knew only the sparkling *Symphonic Suite* taken from the ballet, which was first performed in Cologne in November, 1926.

NEW STORMS: DEFEAT—REVOLUTION— REACTION

THE Hapsburg Empire collapsed; and on 16th November, 1918, Hungary was proclaimed a Republic. Count Károlyi came to power, and wished to introduce social reform, but these plans were frustrated by his frightened friends. Meanwhile the military defeat had produced its usual aftermath—privation, a devaluation of the currency —and there were revolutionary outbreaks. At this point, Béla Kun, former journalist, former political prisoner and a friend of Lenin founded the Hungarian Communist Party. He and his partisans were arrested, but the disturbances, far from ending, now spread to the countryside. There were troubles on the frontiers as well: the Serbian, Rumanian and Czechoslovak armies invaded the border provinces. Béla Kun, as head of a powerful party, was released from prison. He carried with him the hopes of a large part of the nation—and certainly those of the intellectuals and artists, Bartók and his friends, who were ready to help him as best they could. Bartók was a socialist in his own way—a way which sprang from his deep affection for the oppressed country folk—and he had everything to hope for from a new order which would break the hold of the conservative middle class, which showed itself both frivolous and sluggishly apathetic to all the new currents in art

From Rákoskeresztur, in June 1919, Bartók's wife wrote to his mother, dwelling in particular on the black market and the difficulties of finding food. Bartók himself added a postcript describing their departure from Budapest.

"For the time being, here we are once more out of the capital, and contemplating a relatively serene horizon. When we got here, I filled in an application for a 'quiet' apartment in Buda. But that has not yet been arranged. Meanwhile there have been projects for the foundation of a Music Museum. Kunffy had even signed the application, but at the last moment we thought of a better solution: the creation, within the framework of the present museum, of an autonomous folk-music section. I would become its director . . . with Márta and another woman as assistants, then a typist and one or two clerks. The business is already in official hands, and will be confirmed in a few days. . . . It is possible that the new music section will be housed in a palace already commandeered—on St. Margaret

Quay, near the head of Buda bridge, the suspension bridge—on the ground floor of which there would be a flat for the director. In that case we should move in there. But it's difficult to know what to do for the best, since the food situation is certainly better here. One can get milk . . . Márta has already told you of that, and of our keeping chickens! On the other hand, in the flat below us, they have put a working-class family, Slovak agricultural labourers, who make a great deal of noise at times. . . .

"Dohnányi, myself and Zoltán form, as counsellors assisting Reinitz, the political commissar for music, a musical directorate—though we are assisting not on a political basis but purely as experts in music. This activity leads to a great deal of friction, on the one hand with the musicians' 'trade union', on the other higher up, so that we have already once contemplated resigning. Reinitz left for Vienna three weeks ago and it seems that he is unable to come back yet; not the slightest news from him. Of course, great musical reforms are in preparation, but the political situation is too disturbing, it is impossible to work well or with serious concentration. Reinitz's absence at this moment is very annoying. He was one of the few people capable of nipping unjustified and impossible schemes in the bud. Which is why our friends of the musical trade union speak as if they'd like to hang him. Who knows when the ballet, *The Wonderful Mandarin*, will be put on? . . . However, Galafrès would like to produce it."

The internal situation in Hungary grew worse, the pressure of foreign armies grew more intense; Béla Kun declared war on the invaders. At Szeged the revolutionary government armed a few columns. On the 6th of August the counter-revolutionaries and the foreigners entered Budapest after a rapid campaign; Béla Kun fled, the Archduke Joseph was proclaimed Regent, but, being regarded with suspicion by the Allies, was replaced by Admiral Horthy. To the revolutionary excesses of the Left there succeeded the counter-revolutionary excesses of the Right. In the musical world in particular there were purges, dismissals, general uneasiness, and yet still new plans. Only a month after the arrival of the counter-revolutionaries in Budapest, Kodály, as assistant director of the Conservatoire, was asking for six months' holiday with pay for Bartók:

"September, 1919.
"It is a matter of first-rate importance that Bartók, the most eminent composer in our country, recognized throughout Europe, should recover his full capacity for work. I consider it as a circumstance worthy of consideration that in twelve and a half years of official service he has never asked for a long leave, though he has had to struggle against bad health for a long time. Over and above his work as a teacher, he has accomplished during the past ten to twenty years, both as a pianist and as a collector of folk-music, work of such great importance, work also so arduous, that he would

I

urgently need to take care of himself and rest even if
the physical efforts which he has made and the
serious privations which he has endured in the last
few years and months had not weakened his constitution."

(Extract from a minute preserved in the archives
of the Budapest Conservatoire).

The request was granted. But all was not well in
the Budapest musical world, and on 23rd October,
1919, Bartók describes a distressing situation:

"Dohnányi was recently suspended for a year.
Thereupon, fourteen professors went on strike. After
a few days, however, two decided to break the strike,
at which the others also returned to work. And now
the whole thing is coming to a standstill. The
disciplinary investigation of Zoltán and the others
is getting nowhere; the whole thing seems to have
been a farce. Naturally they are getting their full
salary, the only difference is that they are not
working for it; in short, they are better off than the
professors who are not under disciplinary investiga-
tion. In my own case, I am still waiting and
waiting. As long as we are stuck here, in a state of
siege, it is impossible to budge. But—in so far as it
has been possible—I have been inquiring about the
possibilities of making a success of things in three
other countries. For here it is possible to keep
alive, more or less; but it will not be possible to work
here, that is to say to work at what I want—folk-
music studies—for at least ten years. In short,
I want to study folk-music abroad. There is no point

in my remaining here; and if it is not possible to live on folk-music abroad, well . . . one can just as well go on teaching in Vienna as in Budapest, for there, there are at least good musical institutions—orchestras, an opera house and so on . . . everything that they are setting about ruining here by driving away the best, the unique personalities: Tango, Dohnányi, etc. . . .

"In a word, I am not having any trouble here, nobody is persecuting me—not because they have absolutely not the least reason to do so (that's a kind of argument they despise here, now) but because they wouldn't dare. . . . The three foreign places I had in mind are: Transylvania, Vienna and Germany. An 'emigré' music teacher has taken to Germany all my works on folk-music (on Hungarian, Rumanian and Arabic music) in German transla-tion, and is going to try and say a word on my behalf there. Transylvania is what I would most like myself; for me it would be almost like Hungary, or half Hungary; of all ancient Hungary, it is in fact the land that I like best. I have just learned an interesting thing. Tango has been invited to Rumania by the Rumanian Minister of Culture to work in Transylvania. An official was sent to him with the invitation, and this official made a passing allusion—as if to help Tango to make up his mind—to *my* intention of settling in Transyl-vania! Tango is off there to reconnoitre the terrain. I am awaiting his return with curiosity. . . ."[1]

---

[1] Fragment of a letter from Bartók to his mother.

For Bartók the atmosphere of this time was one of
lassitude, of sadness at separating from his mother,
isolated in Pressburg by the Czech army, and above
all, of the general poverty reigning everywhere.
In another letter to his mother, he wrote: "I
have tried to get a visa for Pressburg, but the
Hungarian authorities will not grant me one. . . .
What goes on in the heads of these latest wielders of
power is a riddle to simple mortals like myself; I fear
only that there may be some horrible plans afoot.
But, in short, we shall see.

"You ask me what I have been up to? Nothing
in particular. I am still on leave till the end of
December; then I shall ask for a prolongation,
which no doubt they will be glad to grant me.
Mr. Hubay had made his solemn entry into the halls
of the National Conservatoire of Music—he
apparently himself furnished the 'triumphal march'
with which this event was accompanied—and has
been spreading himself left and right in interviews
with all sorts of newspapers. Thus, for instance, he
declared a fortnight ago in the columns of the
Budapesti Hirlap that he was 'absolutely relying on
Dohnányi and Bartók to support him in his great
task'; recently, on the other hand, he declared in
Az Ujsàg that I could not be expected to interest
myself in piano-teaching; a special post would have
to be created for me that would enable me to enrich
the national musical culture freely, and at my leisure.
That is all that I know and nothing more, for
of course I haven't met Hubay yet. But you can see

from all this that against me personally there hasn't been anything in the least like persecution. You know that for a long time I have been wanting to give up teaching and take another post, for instance in a museum; people like Hubay know this too, and it is possibly of something of this sort that they're thinking. Independently of this, I am making other plans, but naturally I shall not give up the post I have here until I have something absolutely certain and assuredly better elsewhere. When I say 'better' I am not thinking of personal material advantages but of the possibilities of work. The wretched conditions prevailing here certainly make it very questionable whether the State, with the best will in the world, can provide me with the money necessary for buying six hundred phono-graphic cylinders a year and for the incidental expenses of collecting folk-music. Before the war, that amounted to three crowns a cylinder, 1800 crowns in all; with the present value or rather non-value of the crown, multiply three by 20 and say 60 crowns a cylinder, or in round figures 36,000 crowns! ! That's the greatest bother and the greatest obstacle! For the time being, certainly we must wait.

"Thank you very much for the sugar; with what a rapt gaze we watched the glittering cubes with their dazzling whiteness pour out of the parcel, it's years since we've seen any. . . .

"Still no news about the disciplinary investiga-tion of Zoltán and the others. As one might expect, they are awaiting the outcome quite calmly, and up to now have been drawing their full salaries, without doing any work.   All work at the ethnographical museum has been suspended for lack of coal!''

IMPROVISATIONS FOR PIANO; SONATAS FOR VIOLIN AND PIANO

THERE was still one consolation: the fruits of Bartók's folk-music researches during the war at Beszterce-bánya, Ehed and elsewhere.   From these, Bartók took many of the elements which went to make up his *Improvisations* for the piano.

The *Improvisations* must be considered as the extreme point in the evolution of the piano works. In them, Bartók gave his inspiration full reign. Based on peasant tunes, sometimes humorous in character, they are in fact a technical sublimation of the preceding transcriptions of folk-songs.   The fruit of ripe reflection, they are written in a rhapsodic form which incorporates variations linked to each other by developments in which counterpoint plays a clearly defined role.

Next Bartók turned his attention to two *Sonatas for Violin and Piano*.   On these he was to spend two years, from 1921 to 1923—an unusually long period for an artist so quick to impose a final shape on his work.   But no doubt it was necessary.   Claude Debussy, another subtle explorer of the sonata form, once said, ''This kind of music demands a special alchemy, to which one must sacrifice one's cherished tranquillity."

These two sonatas are as directly linked to each other as night and day. The first provides the second with a number of ideas; and the second in its first movement, a rhapsodic fantasy in *parlando-rubato* style, and its second, a finale in *tempo-giusto* rhythm, whose varied inflections of melodic line and movement clearly betray their folk origins, seems a kind of reaction, at once instinctive and unconscious, to the first, a kind of denial of it. This second sonata thus illustrates the Bartókian dualism, that flux and reflux to which I have already alluded. It has not won favour with all critics, even though they are forced to acknowledge the consummate skill of its rhythmical construction.

For my own part, however, I greatly prefer the second sonata to the first. The first is admittedly more interesting from a technical point of view and in relation to the history of music, but it also abounds in rather dry, boring passages, for which the third and last movement, with its dancing charm and robust mood, hardly compensates. It is, I repeat, remarkably interesting for its curious examples of augmentation and diminution of the rhythmic values of the themes in their re-exposition, for the ultra-chromatic melodic lines of the piano accompaniment followed by their concentration in two chords, for the original innovation of entrusting to the violin a line containing all the sounds complementary to those found in the piano chord that sustains them, and for a number of other features.

Thus, whatever reservations I may make, Bartók's *First Sonata for Violin and Piano* is certainly not a work that one must class as a failure. It has too many lessons to teach us. But it is a work of discovery, a reconnaissance in force over new territories, the organization of which was to come later.

INFLUENCES ON BARTÓK

IT is in relation to those two sonatas, especially in relation to the first, that Bartók has been accused of being too much influenced by Schönberg. There had been little objection taken to his love for Debussy and the lessons he had learned from Stravinsky, since the techniques of these two Masters combined to strengthen in him the expression of his own native music. The admiring nationalism of those who saw in Bartók and Kodály the glories of Hungarian national feeling could absorb French and Russian influences. But what were they to think when their director of conscience seemed to have been converted to an Austro-German view of art? To them, that seemed—if not treason—at least desertion.

In plain fact, Bartók appears to have studied Alban Berg much more than Arnold Schönberg, for the complex romanticism à la Mahler and the

Viennese impressionism of the composer of *Wozzeck* was much more in line with his own earliest cultural background than the aggressive expressionist dialectic of the author of *Pierrot Lunaire* (there is, after all, a fundamental stylistic difference between Berg and Schönberg). "That is not *our* music," cried the disciples of the great Arnold, when leaving the first performance of Alban Berg's *Violin Concerto.* Many reflections and turns of phrase in Bartók's work bear witness to Berg's influence—it can be discerned, for instance, in certain lyrical moments of the quartets and the *Violin Concerto.*

But to understand the part played in Bartók's work by such opposite tendencies of the age, we must remember the search for synthesis which is the permanent substratum of that work. Bartók sought to synthesize personal elements—his inspiration and his technique—with elements external to himself —the Hungarian folk-song and the technical innovations of contemporary masters. That is why we see Bartók's musical idiom, fashioned to begin with by teachers for whom Wagner and Brahms were gods, change and evolve partly through spiritual encounters with Strauss, Debussy, Schönberg, Stravinsky, Alban Berg, Hindemith. Have these composers—whose equal he is—imposed a part of their personalities on his, have they marked certain pages with their signature: in short, have they really had "an influence", as that term is generally understood?

No. Bartók absorbed their lessons in the same

way and in the same spirit as Ravel absorbed those of Debussy. He was too powerful, too exclusive a personality to become a disciple in the strict sense. Between his ballet, *The Wonderful Mandarin* and Debussy's *Jeux*, which seems to me its invisible model, between his *Violin Concerto* and that of Alban Berg, of which it is an undoubted consequence, there is the same difference as between the conclusion of the *Marche au Supplice* in Berlioz's *Symphonie Fantastique* and the peroration of Strauss's *Till Eulenspiegel*, which is directly derived from it, or between the first bars of the prelude of the ballet version of Ravel's *Mother Goose* and the introduction of the *Sacre du Printemps*—first presented at the Théâtre des Champs Elysées, 28th May, 1913—though the conception, the atmosphere and the orchestral principles of the second are the result of a close textual study of the first.

In fact, the synthesis of the various technical discoveries of great contemporary composers which Bartók alone has attempted to bring into existence is not only a synthesis but a sublimation. It enriched his personality, it freed him. This is what the eminent musical scholar, Bartók's friend, Constantin Brailoiu, technical director of the International Archives of Folk-Music at Geneva, expressed with rare felicity and conciseness, "Impressionism, polytonalism, atonalism, motorism: Bartók has passionately lived through all these revolutions and reshaped, as it were, for his own use, with his own rich resources, *all* systems."

INTERNATIONAL SUCCESS

WE can date Bartók's international success as a composer from the year 1922, at which we have now arrived. Everywhere his career as a virtuoso-composer took him, he was received with interest and consideration, as these extracts from letters to his mother, written in March, 1922, clearly show.

"Aberystwyth is a little university town of about ten thousand inhabitants where I am giving a concert this evening. The day before yesterday in London, in the house of the Hungarian 'minister' —or consul?—a 'private concert' organized by the Arányis. Though the public were not present, there appeared next day in *The Times* a very favourable criticism. But, even before that, my arrival had been announced in advance in the *Daily Telegraph* and *Daily Mail* and in all the musical journals. They were awaiting me with great interest and gave me a really warm welcome. I am giving a public concert in London on the 24th of March, the organizer has undertaken to bear the risk of loss. The day before yesterday's private concert earned me thirty pounds. I am going to play twice for a family party—ten pounds each time—and here at Aberystwyth I receive fifteen pounds, of which ten pounds net will remain, as my journey here and back to London will not cost me more than five pounds, and here I am the guest of an amiable

household. I haven't yet spent a halfpenny on anything—and as in Paris, in addition to this, I will
pick up 1,500 francs in all, it seems that I may
bring a fair amount of money home with me. . . ."

"It is rather a striking fact that the first private
concert—that of the 14th March—should have
had such long notices in the papers. *The Times* has
spoken of it again. I enclose the notice, try to take
it to A.'s, there may be somebody there who can
translate it for you. It's a great thing when the
papers are busy with my arrival as if it were an
extraordinary event! I wouldn't really have hoped
for it. I have been introduced to an enormous
number of people. I was at a very 'chic' party the
other night—nothing but musicians and critics—
at a rich woman singer's. I played something there
too. To-day I lunched with some Frenchmen.
I have to speak now French, now English—sometimes German—I get through it as well as I can,
but this continual changing of languages completely confuses me. . . ."

On 3rd April, he left for Paris at the invitation
of Henri Prunières, the founder-editor of the
Revue Musicale. The welcome he received remained
unforgettable.

"Dear Mama,

"Yes, I got your postcard. It's rather a long
time since I've written, but I've not been able to.
The concert of the 8th went off very well. Afterwards, there was a dinner at Prunières', at which
there were more than half of 'the best composers

in the world', namely Ravel, Stravinsky, Szyman-owsky, and some young Frenchmen—famous ones —whom you do not know. Most of the composers were very much taken with the *Violin Sonata* but not less so with the playing of Jelly (Arányi, a pupil of Bartók) who surpassed herself this evening. The concert was at five; in the evening after dinner, we played the sonata once again at Prunières' before the select society mentioned above. Prunières says I must come back to Paris next year; he will try to find me about three thousand francs' worth of engagements—out of which I will have about 1,500 francs net profit. I am dining to-day with some Hungarians, the Hungarian Ambassador in Paris will be there. There have been fewer critical notices in the papers here—about four in all. But there is to be a long article in the Easter Monday number of *Le Temps*—perhaps you might get hold of a copy somewhere."

In 1923, Bartók had further successes. He visited Czechoslovakia, Holland, England and Paris again. There was even a Bartók Week in Berlin. In March of that year, he wrote:

"Dear Mama and Aunt Irma,

"I got your postcard yesterday and I am glad you are both well. Yes, I spent the 25th alone, which is to say I went to lunch with the Zoltáns. Certainly, I am working away, but I also go for a walk when I can. Now the concert for the 5th of April at Kassa is definitely fixed—an evening of sonatas with Waldbauer. The Dutch business is

equally certain: Amsterdam on the 27th, Rotterdam
the 28th, Utrecht the 29th, and perhaps a concert
at the Hague. And I have just received an invitation
to England for May, for the moment for three
concerts only, but as I will be in Holland then,
it will be worth while visiting England even for
three concerts. This will enable us to make ends
meet; Hertzka writes me that he has been planning
for next year in Vienna something similar to the
Bartók Week in Berlin. But, as he writes, they will
organize it better. You must come, too!

"The Berlin concerts have created a great
sensation. . . . In the *Pester Lloyd* there was an
article of a column and a half, also by Selden, in
a much warmer tone than his Prague notice. I
shall send it to you. All my love."

The next year, 1924, he again toured the same
countries. In 1925, he visited Italy and Sicily.

Meanwhile, flattering invitations piled up. They
would have turned many people's heads, but not
Bartók's. In May, 1926, he wrote to his mother:
"I got a card yesterday according to which 'The
President of the Council of Royal Hungarian
Ministers and Countess István Bethlen' ask me to
tea on Tuesday at 10 p.m. Fancy what a treat I
find this! Just a year ago the same thing happened,
and I got out of it on some excuse. I don't know
what to do now. I find this sort of social round a
bore."

In 1927, Bartók visited Russia and then New
York, where he played at the Carnegie Hall, with

the Philharmonic Orchestra conducted by Mengelberg, his *Rhapsody* for piano and orchestra. The following year he made a return trip to the States, taking in Holland on the way, and with the Cincinnati Symphony Orchestra, conducted by Fritz Reiner, gave the first performance of his *First Piano Concerto*.

It was during this American tour that the Pro Musica Association organized the first concert entirely devoted to Bartok's chamber music. Bartók and his compatriot Szigeti were the performers. Bartók returned to Europe by way of South America and in Brazil met Villa-Lobos, on whose work he was to have a lasting influence. In 1929 he visited Russia again, then Switzerland; and from this last trip a warm friendship grew up between him and that most talented of patrons and conductors, Paul Sacher.

In 1931, he was at Geneva, invited by the League of Nations as Hungary's delegate to the Congress of Humanistic Sciences; he sat between Gilbert Murray and Paul Valéry.

In 1932, he confronted the great Parisian public at the Salle Pleyel where, with the Paris Orchestral Society under Pierre Monteux, he gave the unforgettable first performance of his *First Concerto for Piano and Orchestra*.

Thus the years of travel went by. Bartók's reputation continued to grow, and in 1936, the big London music publishers, Boosey and Hawkes, offered him an advantageous contract. In 1937,

he was on the road again. Paris saw him once
more in 1938, and again in 1939, on the occasion
of the first performance of the *Sonata for Two
Pianos and Percussion*, and of important fragments
from *Mikrokosmos*. In the same year, 1939, he was
welcomed again in the United States; and in 1940,
he voluntarily exiled himself there. He died there
five years later.

BARTÓK AS VIRTUOSO

IN his concert tours, Bartók usually arranged it
so that Paris should hear the first performance of
his new works. That was his delicate way of paying
the debt of gratitude which he felt he owed to that
little republic of French and foreign composers
known as the École de Paris. Nevertheless, the
modesty of his financial resources forced him also
to plan programmes which, while being certainly of
a high musical standard, would appeal to a wider
and more popular audience than members of the
avant-garde alone. He made a virtue of this necessity
by choosing either the lesser known works of the
great Masters, or those which had been distorted
by the interpretation of megalomaniac virtuosi.
The composers in his repertoire included Scarlatti,
Bach, Handel, Couperin, Mozart, Beethoven,
Chopin, Liszt, Richard Strauss (from the latter,
astonishing and even to-day almost unknown
piano transcriptions of his symphonic poems),
Debussy and Ravel. These were his favourites.

In addition, he played works by a number of his contemporaries: Kodály, Stravinsky, Schönberg and Hindemith.

As for Bartók's special qualities as a pianist, foremost among them was a transcendent sense of phrasing, comparable to that of the very greatest international artists. Of it, Constantin Brailoiu once said: "He dismembered the musical argument piece by piece, laying its most tenuous articulations bare, like an X-ray which under the flesh illuminates the delicate details of the skeleton. Thus, in his hands, illuminated in depth, over-familiar masterpieces were born anew and as if heard for the first time, as if by some magic spell."

There were, indeed, some people who criticized Bartók's style, especially those faithful to the idea of "purely intuitive interpretation"—that false notion of a permanent state of grace inherited from the Romantics. But there were many others who at once leapt vigorously to the defence of Bartók whenever such criticisms were uttered.

Bartók's second quality as a pianist was a tone at once rich and precise—a range of shades of colour so exactly differentiated that it might be compared to that of Alexander Borowsky. Bartók's solo records made in Italy before 1939 do not convey these qualities, because of mediocre recording techniques. His most faithful recording is the record of the *Sonata for Two Pianos and Percussion*, in which the second piano part is played by his second wife, Ditta Pásztori.

K

To explain Bartók's technique as a pianist, we have to remember that he was primarily a composer. On the other hand, his gifts as a pianist were invaluable to him during the process of composition. If he had not been himself a pianist, he would have come up against a double difficulty: first it would not have been easy for him to find a sufficiently devoted interpreter of his works, and he would thus have made a much more belated impression on the awareness of his contemporaries; and secondly, the fundamentally harmonic character of the keyboard, what one might call its "harmonic gravity", preserved him from the dizzy fascinations of pure intellectualism, from hurtling into those abysses discovered by Désiré Pâques, organized by Arnold Schönberg, and turned into a dogma by Ernst Krenek and René Leibowitz.

In a word, I do not think it is an exaggeration to say that without his practice in the art of the piano, Bartók would have found it difficult to resist the distortions of theories that become irrational by pushing reason too far, and would not have been able to lead us into the luminous realm of of pure music.

BARTÓK'S SECOND MARRIAGE (1923)

BARTÓK found teaching the piano a hateful task. It is true that in 1907 he had decided to accept Thomán's post at the Budapest Conservatoire, but then he had a family to support: he had been married for two years to his first wife, Márta, by whom he had a son also called Béla (who is now an engineer). Nevertheless, he submitted himself cheerfully to his new duties, and even edited a number of classical works with a commentary. Thus we have the two series of J. S. Bach's *Well-Tempered Clavier* prefaced and analysed by one of the most acute musical intelligences of modern times, and a progressive piano method, a kind of involuntary preface to that monument of graduated technique, *Mikrokosmos*, which he began to compile in 1907. But as soon as his engagements as a virtuoso enabled him to support his family, Bartok handed in his resignation.

It was during his time as a teacher that Bartók met the young woman who became his second wife: Ditta Pásztori, one of his pupils in his class at the Conservatoire. In 1923, a divorce was arranged on a friendly basis between himself and Márta, but it was preceded by a period of distress. In his letters to his mother during this period, a curious note of resignation breaks through.

"Márta and Béla have kept very well here," he wrote from Radvavy in August, 1923. "We have gone out for many walks together. To tell you the truth, I should have gone off to a chalet up in the mountains much sooner, but I stayed down below so as to be with them, and to work on my latest composition. It is pity that they can't stay here longer, but Béla will be just as well off at Szöllös, and Márta too for that matter. They

like it there very much. And in the present circumstances, contrast too has a special value. Well,
to-day I am off to the mountains at last, but I shall
only be able to stay there about five days. I've
almost finished the new score (he is referring to the
Fourth Suite for Full Orchestra, known under the
name of *Dance Suites*). I am leaving on August 20th
for Pest where I still have quite a number of things
to arrange before the end of the month when the
marriage takes place. I am very glad that Márta's
letter has calmed you a little, for it troubled me
that you were so saddened. Of course, I do understand your apprehension: but you must try, all
the same, to resist it as far as possible, so long as
you do not see the situation clearly. I really believe
that it is going to be all right this way, or even
better than it has been so far. In fact, it is only for
Márta that it will be much worse, and that is the
only thing that saddens me. So much so that I
would not have demanded this sacrifice of her, I
should not have been able to do so even though
human reason commanded it. But it is she herself
who has committed me to this complete change,
and I couldn't refuse for it was not only myself who
was involved. Little Béla has taken the whole thing
quite calmly; it is rather the special nature of the
situation that impresses him. I hope that you also
will gradually take a calmer view.

"I have still much to do to the new composition
—you know, of course, that I am talking of the
Orchestral Dances that are to be given in Budapest

on 19th November at a concert of Gela's. The score must be ready by the end of August so that they can do the orchestral parts in Vienna."

The following letter, written ten days after the marriage, in September, 1923, shows Bartók feeling the relief that follows on the accomplishment of a perilous task.

"I got your postcard, and we thank you for your good wishes. We are beginning to get straight, but we still have much to do and new acquisitions to make. So far, everything is going well and in good order; Ditta is a skilful housekeeper. In the morning she looks after the house and helps in the kitchen too, where she is also very clever. In the afternoon there are lots of other things for her to do, the piano, etc. . . . Turning to my own affairs, I must tell you that I now have a monthly salary of 600,000 crowns, which is quite enough to meet our household expenses. . . . Márta is very well, she has put on twelve pounds—particularly while she was staying with Elsa—and I am really glad about that. She is also taking a cheerful view of things. Work begins at the Conservatoire to-morrow: the entrance examinations—ugh! I have never liked them.

"Many kisses for you and Aunt Irma."

IMAGINARY FOLK-MUSIC (1923)

THE third orchestral suite, known under the title of *Dance Suite*, at which Bartók was working at this

period placed him definitively among the ten or
twelve international Masters who set their stamp
on a given musical epoch. In Germany alone
it was played fifty times within twelve months. It
had been commissioned by the Hungarian Government for the commemoration of the jubilee of the
union of Buda with Pest, and it was performed
at a festival directed by Dohnányi, after a brilliant
Solemn Overture by the latter, and that masterpiece
of contemporary music, the *Psalmus Hungaricus* of
Kodály. After twenty years of struggle, the three
friends were together again in the same triumph.

In the five movements of the *Dance Suite*, with the
recurring refrain which links them together, Bartók
has provided the finest example of what I have
called his imaginary folk-music. All the themes
are based on folk tunes, yet none is an actual folk
tune. But all of them share the deep life of the
Magyar race, and the instrumental setting syn-
thesizes the physical atmosphere of the places from
which that life emanates. In this work Bartók
gives final proof of his genius—for what is genius
but the explicit condensation in a single mind of
ideas that, in an obscure and fragmentary state,
belong to all? The success which greeted this
composition is also a practical demonstration
of the truth of Kodály's words, "To become international, one must first be national, and to be
national, one must be of the people."

Of the thematic material which he had amassed
for the *Dance Suite*, enough remained to compose

another work almost as vast—great artists are prodigal in this fashion. Besides, Bartók was filled with such exaltation at having brought off such a perilously difficult feat that he could not but be tempted to repeat his *tour de force*. Thus, in 1924, the *Village Scenes* for voice and piano came into being (they were orchestrated two years later). The five movements, which depict a Slovak marriage, were in some ways a choral counterpart to, and an aesthetic concentration of the *Two Images* for orchestra of 1910, and of the *Sonatina* for piano of 1915. They have sometimes been compared to Stravinsky's *Noces*, rather imprudently however, if an influence is suggested, since the definitive version of Stravinsky's astonishing composition dates from 1923, and it is improbable that Bartok had any knowledge of it. The spiritual relationship between the two works must spring rather from the fact that when two artists of this calibre embark on a profound treatment of the same subject—in this case both starting with Slavonic folk themes—their work must necessarily have a good deal in common.

CHAPTER FOUR

BARTÓK'S ACHIEVEMENTS IN PURE MUSIC

BETWEEN 1923 and 1926, no further works appeared. It would seem that Bartók was gathering his forces within himself before taking up the pen again, that he was perhaps hesitating for a moment before entering finally into the realm of pure music, like his master, Claude Debussy, when the latter was meditating over his last sonatas. One can imagine him halted on the path of this spiritual quest in that "dark night" which is known not only to the saints but to the great creators of ideas, when the tangible world loses its consistency and is transmuted into symbol.

But the long silence was broken at last, and the result was the *Sonata* for piano. This important work abounds in multiple, often aggressive intentions, forming a dense tissue of sound which may well prove baffling at a first hearing, and which is hardly relieved by an andante consisting of ideas whose contrapuntal play evokes, but at a long remove, impressionist echoes. The two fast movements have such richness of volume that they convey an orchestral atmosphere. The special form of each can often be grasped only in the light of that "rhythmical thematic structure" of which I have already spoken; but one feels in the first movement the almost conscious presence of a Beethoven schema. (Let us always, for that matter, bear in mind when we are examining one of Bartók's works from the point of view of form that his conception of volume in movement had its origins in the last works of Beethoven, and that he drew ultimate conclusions from the quartets and sonatas with variations of the Master of Bonn.)

Turning from this exploration of the richest of harmonic materials, Bartók, obeying the law of compensation that arose from the very duality of his own nature, next set about creating an equal complexity of melodic lines, in a series of compositions in which counterpoint played the dominant role.

The first of these were the *Nine Short Pieces*, in the first four of which the influence of J. S. Bach—and particularly of the *Inventions*—appeared clearly for the first time. In certain of these pieces, No. 6 for example, the polyphonic style even seems to go back to Bach's Italian sources and further yet, to Frescobaldi. The same trend became even more evident in the *Outdoor Music* for piano, which followed. In the *Barcarolle*, for instance, the second of this collection of fourteen pieces, polyphony and harmony are so intimately interdependent that it is hard to say which of them was the basis of the idea. With this work, we find ourselves once more in a familiar atmosphere—the atmosphere of the *Bagatelles* of 1908, but now evoked by an intelligence that has greatly gained in lucidity.

This new mastery can also be seen in the *First Concerto* for piano and orchestra, which also came out in 1926, one of the most fertile years in Bartók's career. Though rarely played, it is a masterpiece. It was, for that matter, unanimously recognized as such by the German critics when Bartók presented it in the following year, under the direction of Wilhelm Furtwängler, during the Frankfurt Music Week.

The counterpoint of lines and rhythms gives the first and third movements of this work a clearly traditional form, variety and solidity, and sets off the unforgettable, disturbing andante, in which the piano converses almost solely with the percussion instruments, which respond to the superimposed developments of the piano lines with the rhythmic schemata on which these lines are based. Impressionism still adds patches of light and colour. Certain sections are firmly bi-tonal. Nevertheless, the composer maintains a firm hold on a latent harmony (in E, for the first and third movements, in G for the second), thanks to the insistent and sustained pedal notes entrusted by turns to the orchestra and the soloist. With this monumental use of constantly increasing tensions, Bartók went even further than he himself had foreseen when he wrote to his friend von der Müll, "In the last few years, I have been much occupied with music written before

Bach, and I believe there are traces of this to be perceived in the *Concerto* for piano." That, indeed, is the miraculous effect of true culture. It frees the artist of genius from the conventions of his own age, and at the same time, instead of imprisoning him in the past, opens the way for him to things that have not yet been said.

So it has always been. For instance, it was to a profound study of Couperin and of the ancestor of all French descriptive music, Jannequin, that Claude Debussy owed his originality. And it was Paul Hindemith's painstaking work on the old Italians that freed him from the tutelage of Max Reger.

THIRD QUARTET (1927) AND *FOURTH QUARTET* (1928)

BARTÓK'S recent contrapuntal experiments now led him to a musical form in which the play of lines is more necessary than anywhere else and facilitated by the nature of that form. Thus, in his *Third String Quartet* of 1927, he composed a work for which he shared with Casella the prize given by the city of Philadelphia for the best piece of chamber-music. The prize was well deserved, for in the two parts of this work in cyclic form, with its contrapuntal elaborations and its astonishing poly-rhythms, there is an art which confounds the senses; the search for orchestral timbres foreign

to the strings and the chromatic stretti of the
finale show an unheard-of skill. The stretti foreshadow the sublime fugue of the first and last
movements of the *Music for Strings and Percussion*.
It is another cause for wonder that the two parts of
this quartet are linked to each other by a series of
transitional artifices containing thematic superimpositions of prodigious ingenuity. The composition is a prolongation of certain experiments
visible in the second *Sonata* for violin; one often
finds, for instance, melodic lines arising from a
harmonic dissonance which subsumes them, and
sinking back there again, as well as different
variations of the same idea marching side by side
in a unity imposed by the general rhythm of the
work.

René Leibowitz says very justly: "In fact this
emerges as the first of a whole series of works, in
the course of which Bartók will explore ever more
deeply an architectonic principle founded on the
unity of all parts of the same work. This principle,
which goes back to the last quartets of Beethoven,
had already had a masterly recrudescence in the
famous Schönbergian attitude of 'durchkomp-
onieren' (through-composing') as it is embodied
in the two first quartets and the *Chamber Symphony*
of the Viennese master."

I have purposely quoted the second as well as
the first part of that paragraph. It states a significant fact . . . and reminds us of the great danger
with which, not perhaps the attitude of Schönberg

himself, but the dogmatizing rage of his lesser followers, has confronted contemporary music in general, and that of Bartók in particular. Their intellectualism systematizes the melodic line in such a strict and *a priori* fashion that it becomes dessicated by being severed from its instinctive sources; it further distorts the melodic line by an arbitrary, complicated and finally incoherent notion of musical space, since the musical volume produced by serial dodecaphonism is the mere fortuitous result of linear superimpositions.

But what are the musical experiments of the Masters except groping gestures that seek to delimit a volume of which the artist already has an obscure presentiment? The lines, the melodies that manifest these volumes are only secondary in creative time; and to wish to give them a primary role is spiritual perversion. That is why serial dodecaphonism is hurtful, and why Bartók, a sane and healthy artist living the normal life of human-kind, always rejected it. Thus, he was able to stretch out to an extraordinary degree the network of lines enclosing the volume, and cover the latter with a kind of intellectual chain mail, without our deeper psychic intuition losing the notion of the fundamental volume itself.

Nevertheless, in his works between 1926 and 1928, Bartók tested the resistance of his musical material to the utmost. This is often evident in the *Fourth String Quartet*, composed in 1928. Before embarking on it, and after finishing the *Third*

String Quartet, Bartók's only other compositions had
been the three *Rondos* for piano (of which the first
actually dates from 1916). Their brilliant and all
too little known pages are full of delightful outbursts of humour.

The *Fourth String Quartet* shows us a Bartók whose
power of architectonic conception and intelligence
in applying his conceptions equal those of his
model, Beethoven. The five parts of the work form
a whole and the meaning of each part is perceived
only in relation to the others.

The scheme of the work can be summed up
thus: A (sonata allegro), B (scherzo), C (andante),
B¹ (a scherzo whose thematic material derives from
B), A¹ (a finale on themes from A). The central
movement, towards which the two first flow, and
from which the last two set off, powerfully contains,
in summary formulation, the ideas of the whole
work which can thus be schematized in three
driving tempos: the first A and B, the second C,
the third A¹ and B¹. Thus we see that the *Fourth
Quartet* is a sort of amplification of the third in
three parts, the first fast, the second slow, the third
fast.   Here we lay bare the originality of the
Bartókian notion of form: in the last analysis it is
a sonata allegro (the form A, B — B¹, A¹) stretched
to the limits of the intelligible. Thus the work
with which we are concerned might be schematized
thus: A, first idea—B, second idea—C (development of A and B), followed by the developments
of B and A, the sum total of these developments

leading us to B^1 and A^1, the classical formula for the "sonata allegro". This transposition of the classical formula into the modern form, by amplifications well within the Beethoven tradition, must be borne in mind when we seek to understand the architectonic conception of many of Bartók's works. The young modern composer could profit by meditating on this quartet with its forms at once clear, complex and above all tested by the experience of the past; to be "in the tradition" is not simply to take formulae from the past but to make them alive and self-transcendent.

This is an impassioned work—some have even called it romantic in feeling. However that may be, the ebullient prestissimo of the muted violins in the second movement, the lyrical tone of the ideas of the third movement, reflected almost sarcastically as in a distorting glass in the fourth, and the variations and rhythmic imitations of the first and last movements—all these have a power to sweep the listener into willing surrender, so that it is only later that one is able to analyse the tendencies of the work as a whole. I know excellent musicians who, though they may be irritated by the aesthetic that underlies the *Fourth String Quartet*, cannot help going back to it again and again—an obvious proof of its vitality.

This vitality is due to three factors: first, to a rhythm that can pass from calm to fury with no rupture of its logical continuity; secondly, to the construction of a tonal accompaniment to that rhythm which has an orchestral richness; and thirdly, to a tonal liaison between the movements and to a repetition of general tonalities in a classically devised schema. The first movement is in the atmosphere of C (tonic), the second in that of E (the dominant of the parallel tonic, which plays here the part of the alternate tonic), the third is imprecise but moves round the dominant functions of the first and second. The theme of the fourth movement derives from tonality of A-flat, taken as a function of the sub-dominant, and the fifth takes us back to C. The schema of the tonal plan is therefore classically orthodox: tonic—dominant—sub-dominant—tonic.

The preceding observations throw a particularly vivid light on Bartók's nature: he was not a revolutionary, but an evolutionary.

THE *CANTATA PROFANA* (1930)

AFTER such a lofty and sustained effort, Bartók needed a rest. As always, he found the freshness and tranquillity necessary to the restoration of his sensibility in his beloved folk-songs and in their corollary, imaginary folk-music.

Thus, the two *Rhapsodies for Violin* came into existence. The first, dedicated to Szigeti, has a form somewhat reminiscent of that of the Second Sonata, for it presents a stylization of the Lisztian aesthetic. There was to have been a version of it for 'cello and orchestra—Bartók had authorized his pupil Géza Frid (now a well-known pianist and composer, and a naturalized Dutchman) to undertake the work—but the Anschluss and with it the breaking-off of relations between Bartók and his Vienna publishing house, made the project abortive.

The second *Rhapsody* was composed in 1929, in the little house in the Budapest suburbs where Bartók used to rest after his tours. It has a charming popular air, and its brilliant, dry orchestration, strongly based on a tonal-modal harmony, reveals an underlying pattern of sober statements in counterpoint. These are linear tissues of the same sort as those found in the twenty harmonizations of Hungarian folk-songs which belong to the same period.

In 1930 appeared Bartók's only major choral work—the *Cantata Profana*. In this work, with its astonishing density, its calm depths of feeling, its close-packed, unfaltering composition, we can see the consequences of Bartók's recent meditations on the *Passions* of J. S. Bach. The sub-title of the *Cantata Profana* is *The Enchanted Stags*. It employs a double choir, a baritone (the father), a tenor (the eldest son), and a normal orchestra. The words are based on a very ancient Rumanian ballad, derived from a folk tale that is still told on the banks of the Volga. The work is divided into three parts: "The Nine Sons", "The Meeting with the Father" and "This was the Legend".

A father had nine sons. They lived together in a

L

wooded mountain district, and were skilled only in hunting. One day they set off to follow the tracks of a herd of deer, and soon came upon the leader of the herd—unknown to them, an enchanted beast. They fired at him and missed, and, as punishment for their sacrilege, were themselves changed into stags. At this, however, they were overjoyed, for they were now able to come and go in absolute freedom. "Our great antlers seek the valleys . . . we drink at the springs. . . ."

The composer treats this first episode in a broad choral-symphonic style, in which the handling of the music seems as densely-woven and harmonious as the Carpathian forests in which the story takes place.

Meanwhile, the father, growing anxious at the absence of his sons, takes his rifle and sets off in search of them. Suddenly, he sees the stags, and shoulders his rifle, but one of them cries out:

"O Father, do not fire, for from our woods we should pierce you and hurl you far away, far across the plains."

"Come back, O my sons, your mother is waiting, she is alone. Come back, the meal is on the table."

"No, our antlers would not pass the door. From now on our hooves shall crush the thyme, from now on we shall drink no more from a cup but from the pure springs; our bounding bodies are made to walk in nakedness."

Some parts of this episode show a wonderful art: the eager rhythm of the introduction, representing the anxious father's quest, the following fugue, the progress from the lowest to the highest registers of the tenor voice from the words, "Do not shoot", to the words, "We should hurl you far away, far across the plains", and the dramatic feeling of the dialogue.

In the third part, the two choirs, now in unison, now alternately, repeat the key sentences from the elder brother's speech and the work concludes with the phrase: "From now on we shall drink at the pure springs."

This Cantata had a secret political meaning. In writing it, Bartók wanted to protest against the limits which the personal power of the Regent Horthy set to individual liberty in Hungary. Such restrictions were always unbearable to a lifelong and intransigent democrat like Bartók. Because it is a homage to liberty, contemporary Hungarian musical scholars like to call it *Our Cantata Profana*. This explains both why the *Cantata Profana* was very rarely performed in Hungary between the wars, and why Bartók had a peculiar tenderness for it.

RETREAT FROM CHROMATICISM:

THE *SECOND CONCERTO* (1930-31)

EARLY in 1931, Bartók completed his *Second Concerto* for piano and orchestra. I myself consider this work has greater importance as an example of

the evolution of Bartók's style, than as a purely
aesthetic achievement. If the hearer has about a
dozen moments of pure pleasure in the balanced
development of the three movements, in the happy
equilibrium between the orchestral and pianistic
masses, and in the often classical manner in which
the themes are sustained by cunning counterpoint, coloured by a skilful use of the percussion
instruments, the professional musician is disconcerted by a certain heterogeneity of style in the
melodic material. This is due to the intrusion of a
neo-classical diatonism within a chromatic framework which is very much modified by comparison
with the chromaticism used by Bartók in other
works written from 1926 onwards. Thus, this work
—which has, I repeat, its own fascination for an
ear unused to the criteria of comparison—can be
considered without injustice by the critic as transitional.

A crisis was taking place in Bartók's creative
consciousness. After the *Fourth Quartet*, he found
himself forced to reject the absurd consequences
of total chromaticism, consequences which force
the disciples of chromaticism to employ a single
series of twelve notes in an invariable order during
the whole course of a piece. This rejection had led
him back towards diatonism, all the more easily
because he had always remained loyal to an
essential harmony, however much he may have
loosened or extended its relations. This attitude,
founded on a fidelity to an order established prior

to all music by the physics of vibration, this submission to the acoustic properties of sonorous bodies, relates Bartók to Paul Hindemith. Some of Hindemith's preoccupations are therefore reflected in some of Bartók's later works, those often described, rather superficially, as "neo-classic".

To sum up: the *Second Concerto* is a compromise, not a synthesis. It is to the admirable *Sonata for Two Pianos and Percussion* what the *Fantasia* for choir, piano and orchestra by Beethoven is to the *Ninth Symphony*: a polymorphous groping forward.

In the *Fantasia*, the active element, the germ, lay not in the orchestral or pianistic but in the choral writing, and more precisely in the twelve bars which sketch out the polyphony still to come of Schiller's *Hymn to Joy*; so in Bartók's *Second Concerto* the germ of future achievement is to be found in the use of the percussion instruments whose rhythmic complexity, multiplicity of timbres, and combinations break rather harshly into a work which as a whole is not deliberately experimental.

To support my thesis of a crisis in Bartok's creative consciousness, I might draw an argument from this fact: during the three years that followed the *Second Concerto* Bartók devoted himself solely to the harmonization of folk-melodies of all kinds. There are the *Hungarian Folk-Songs* for choir (1930), the *Transylvanian Dances* for orchestra (1931)— a very effective composition though soberly conceived—the *Sicules Songs* for male choir (1932), the

Hungarian Peasant Songs (1933), so impressive in their strong and bare orchestration, based on the wind instruments, and whose picturesque corollary is the *Hungarian Folk-Songs* for voice and orchestra (1933).

During these years there was one exception— a piece of pure music, though one which draws many of its elements from authentic folklore—and over this we must linger for some time, though its material is not spectacular. The *Forty-Four Duets* for violin were practically ignored, even by violinists, till they had been recorded. We owe them to a lucky combination of circumstances. In 1931, the distinguished Professor Erich Döflein, who to-day teaches at the University of Freiburg, wrote with his wife a manual for the violin into which, with praiseworthy boldness, he wished to insert certain easy duets written by contemporary composers. Having admired the intelligence of the method of piano teaching which Bartók had previously elaborated in collaboration with Reschofsky, Döflein got into touch with Bartók. The latter promised him everything he wanted, and the first thing he sent him was the forty-fourth duet of the series, *Rumanian Gypsy Dance*. Döflein, finding it difficult, asked for some easier pieces; these, too, were sent. Thus, week by week, the number of duets grew and ended in the famous collection which really comprises forty-five, not forty-four duets, since number 36 has a variant. In the *Forty-Four Duets* there are utter gems (why should

Bartók working on records of Rumanian folk-tunes,
Bucharest, 1934.

the marvellous in music be restricted to the monumental?). Authentic or imaginary folk-songs and dances are presented concisely and treated in a style of free, balanced harmony and counterpoint. I would even commit myself to the statement that, without a deep study of this work, it is impossible to get very far in the analysis of Bartók's larger compositions; the *Forty-Four Duets* offer one a summary of his reactions to harmony, counterpoint and rhythm. They are an introduction, in fact, to the Bartókian method.

THREE MASTERPIECES: 1934–37

(a) THE *FIFTH QUARTET* (1934)

AFTER three years of indecision, the sublimation of the painful conflict between the chromatic and the diatonic—a new expression of that fundamental Bartókian dualism which we have noticed earlier—took place in a series of masterpieces.

The first of these was the *Fifth Quartet*; it was written in a month, between 6th August and 6th September. (And surely such a sudden rush of inspiration is a further proof that there had been a previous inner struggle about techniques, in other words, a crisis.)

We must embark now upon a technical analysis, which should be especially useful in this case, since it will clarify the hearer's mind and prepare him to grasp the content of this work of genius when he has the chance to hear it played by some international quartet. The Hungarian Végh quartet give far and away the best performance of this work, and have specialized in all Bartók's six quartets.

First Movement: "Allegro". The first theme in B-flat already shows all the characteristics of Bartók's style: rhythmical repetition of a note, modes that have many half-tones but are not truly chromatic, imitations and variations of the same internal patterns within quite small intervals, and favourite intervals such as augmented fourths, minor thirds and minor seconds. In an intermediate passage—a short motif with trills—there appears another very important principle: contrary movement, or reversal. The second theme, related to the first by its intervals, but differentiated by its rhythm, leads, as an irregular rhythmic imitation, to the reappearance of the first theme, interspersed with accentuated harmonies. The third theme is calmer: over tied notes and pizzicati, its motifs move up and down in strange modes and pass from one instrument to another. In the development, use is made primarily of the materials of the first theme (in E augmented fourth) to which are joined the rhythms of the second theme, then a variant of the third, with more ample unchromatic intervals and imitations closely packed together in the minor second. The re-exposition is opened with a reversal of the first theme; the third and second themes follow and then the first theme again in contrary movement. A lively coda, with very close reversed imitations, leads just before the end to a repetition of the initial theme of the first movement.

Second Movement: "Adagio molto". After an introduction which is almost evanescent, so tenuous is the musical material (trills, motifs of two notes passing from one instrument to another), we hear a very noble chorale entrusted to the brass instruments; the modal harmonization in perfect chords gives it a hieratic character not without analogies to the movement in the Lydian mode in Beethoven's quartet, Op. 132 (a principle taken up again in Bartók's third concerto). Upon this chorale the violin embroiders a motif in notes which are foreign to its harmony. In the middle section, the play of brief motifs is woven together above a foundation of tremolos and pizzicati, mounts to a crescendo, and after a long descent across the four instruments, leads to a very abbreviated and reversed re-exposition.

Third Movement: "Scherzo alla Bulgarese". What characterizes the Bulgarian rhythms of which Bartók makes much use in this movement is, we should remember, an unequal duration of the musical beat which sometimes contains two quavers, sometimes three. Thus in the first part of the scherzo we have a rhythm in four-four time, in which the last beat contains three quavers, while in the trio, also in four-four time, the first and fourth beats have three quavers.

In the scherzo, the half-tones usual in other movements give way to the more ample intervals of thirds which compose the undulating line of the principal theme. The violins expound it on a basis of pizzicati from the 'cello, and the viola interrupts with a diatonic motif. A second rhythmically contrasting subject supervenes and is not unrelated to certain motifs of the first movement.

The trio, more rapid, leads to a new theme from the first violin, played *ostinato*; under it, first the viola and then the 'cello take up a very simple melody. The violin theme spreads to all the instruments; a crescendo bursts out, followed by a diminuendo, during which the motifs of the scherzo appear in the 'cello; this natural development of the melody of the trio leads to a re-expounding of the scherzo in which Bartók makes an extensive use of the principle of contrary movement.

Fourth Movement: "Andante". A short pizzicato movement passing from one instrument to another leads to a development in which, against a re-iterated base note first on G and then on D, and pizzicati, glissandos and trills, a short expressive violin phrase detaches itself. There is an interruption of tremolos from the four instruments, and then on the same foundation of trills, glissandos and tied notes, a canon between the violin and 'cello is introduced. Then there appears a chromatic motif, expressing a certain agitation; and as a culminating point, against a background of gliding chromatics from the 'cello and viola, there appears an expressive phrase entrusted to the first violin, which the second imitates in canon. A diminuendo leads to a lessening of tension; short explosions subside beneath a very simple mounting and descending line of the violins repeating the harmonies of the chorale of the first movement.

Fifth Movement: "Finale". After a brief introduction of short rippling triplets, the principal theme is expounded by the violins against a rhythmic accompaniment from the two other instruments. It is taken up again in canon; in the sequel all the motifs constituting it undergo a contrapuntal development which leads to a brief re-exposition of the theme in reversed form. An intermediary passage with a rhythmic motif in fifths and seconds built up one upon another, and then a closely-packed chromatic interval, superimposing all the notes of the chromatic scale, lead to the second theme which is expounded in canon, first by the two violins, then by the viola and 'cello, this theme then undergoing every device of contrapuntal development. There is an interruption by the initial triplet passages, then on a rhythmic *ostinato*, the principal theme of the first movement joins in in its turn. Following this, the second theme is briefly recalled in a variant form, and followed by the principal theme canonically expounded with its original forms reversed. The initial rhythmical motif, built up on diatonic chords on this occasion, and a short passage

marked "allegretto con indifferenza", interpose
themselves before the final outburst of a frenzied
coda.

It has no doubt been noticed that the form of
the *Fifth Quartet*, in its rhythmical disposition, is
the inverted reflection of the *Fourth*; in the latter,
two fast movements flank a slow central movement,
in the former it is two slow movements that enclose
a fast middle movement. There the resemblance
comes to an end, for the arrangement and use of the
thematic material in the *Fifth Quartet* does not have
the feeling of a "sonata allegro" but rather of a
Beethoven rondo, expanded to monumental di-
mensions. In fact, the architecture of the *Fifth
Quartet* can be reduced to the following schema:

A: B: C-A^I: D-B^I: E-A^{II}-A.

Its general unity is also reinforced by the presence
of short thematic and rhythmic motifs which can
be found in each of the movements.

To the hearer, the *Fifth Quartet* is notable for its
relaxed quality: the sharp chromaticism of the
Fourth Quartet is rounded off, the furious and
hurtling dance of the allegros, though still rapid,
becomes a graceful game, the pathetic qualities
have been muted into lyricism. In a word, the
colours are, as painters say, "toned down", for the
greater pleasure of the connoisseur. This tone of
relaxation indicates a mastery which at length
knows and is at ease with itself.

After such an intense outburst of creative energy,

Bartók turned for a respite back to folk-songs and dances. He was obeying that same pendulum swing which we have already noted: from pure music to folk-music, then on to pure music, and back to folk-music again.

In 1935 he wrote twenty-seven two- and three-part choruses for women's and children's choirs, and three three-part choruses for male voices—admirable additions to the repertory of contemporary choral music. These were followed by the *Little Suite* for piano, in which many of the sections were based on *parlando-rubato* rhythms, and the whole work breathed a picturesque charm. Indeed, this work, especially in the allegro sections, seems to sum up in essence all the joys of musical creation.

At that time, however, Bartók had little cause for joy. Nazi Germany was on the march; and Bartók, with his deep love of freedom, was not the man to watch that sinister progress without suffering. Furthermore, in his frequent retreats into the countryside, in his friendships with the peasantry of different countries, he had acquired too deep a feeling for the significance of human life not to be distressed by the gathering rumours of war.

He showed both his hatred for the Hitler régime and his love of artistic liberty by a sudden gesture: though not himself a Jew, he demanded that his works should be prominently represented among those of Jewish composers at the exhibition of "degenerate music" organized by the new association of German composers known as the S.T.A. G.M.A.

(b) *MUSIC FOR STRINGS,*
PERCUSSION AND CELESTA (1936)

IT was while all these international tensions were growing more acute, in 1936, that Bartók conceived and completed what is undoubtedly one of the masterpieces of Western music in the present century: the *Music for Strings, Percussion and Celesta.*

The title itself indicates the instruments employed: two string orchestras, piano, harp, celesta, percussion instruments and timpani.

The *First Movement*—"Andante tranquillo"—is a fan-shaped fugue in which the different entries of the subject follow one another in the order of the cycle of fifths, to arrive at the furthest removed key (E-flat). The fugue has this curious characteristic: the first entry of the subject has six chromatic notes, the second six others, which gives us the twelve degrees of the chromatic scale in two entries, and thus a strict adherence to the serial dodecaphonic formula. Bartók doubtless wished to prove that one could employ the full scale of sounds in the manner of Schönberg and his disciples, while in the subsequent composition preserving reason, liberty and a respect for auditory appropriateness. From the tonality of E-flat, once reached, the initial tonality is brought back by abbreviations and an inverted development. Then follows the coda, in which the subject, superimposed on its reversed form, is expounded for the last time over delightful

arpeggios from the celesta which evoke the ghost of
Debussy in a rather unexpectedly philosophical
atmosphere.

The *Second Movement*—"Allegro"—is in the form of
a "sonata allegro". The principal theme is carried
by a rapid rhythm to a development in which the
theme of the first movement reappears. The
concluding re-exposition has this original aspect:
that the initial theme, instead of being presented in
2/4, is presented in 3/8 time.

The *Third Movement*—"Adagio"—is surely one of
the strangest fragments of all known music. It
contains three elements:

(A) A rhythm at first accelerated, then slowing
down on the F of the xylophone, followed by short
passages of viola recitative above the tremolos of
the basses;

(B) An expressive melody for violin and celesta;

(C) A motif of five notes hammered out by all the
sections of the orchestra. The re-exposition is
inverted (that is, B before A). Between the different
parts appear fragments of the theme of the first
movement.

The *Fourth Movement*—"Allegro Molto"—is an
astonishing linking together of dances of folk inspiration leading to an abridged and variant re-exposition of the fugue of the first movement, whose theme
is this time presented diatonically, though it had
been originally presented chromatically. This
philosophical conclusion, retrospectively throwing
light on the memory of the preceding movements,

removes the sense that their brilliant thematic possibilities had never been quite actualized, and integrates them into the general atmosphere.

We see here the form of the "extended rondo" of which Bartók was so fond. The thematic "stanzas", each different, are linked together this time by variations of the first movement which play the part of a refrain and a conclusion:

$$A: B-A^{I}: C-A^{II}: D-A^{II}-A.^{I}$$

This composition is a masterpiece, because elements as disparate as twelve-tone chromaticism, folk-music, diatonic harmonization, linear orchestration and impressionist colouring are co-ordinated into a homogeneous combination which exerts the utmost fascination on the hearer.

(c) SONATA FOR TWO PIANOS AND PERCUSSION (1937)

THE following year, 1937, Bartók wrote his third masterpiece, the *Sonata for Two Pianos and Percussion*, a logical sequence to the key ideas behind its predecessor. It seems, indeed, likely that some of the ideas for this work occurred to Bartók while he was still writing the *Music for Strings*, that he could not find a place for them there, but that their quality was such that he could not bring himself to abandon them after finishing his task. On the other hand, this new work is also in the tradition of the andante of the *First Concerto* and the fast movements of the *Second Concerto*, for the symphonic role of the percussion instruments, outlined in the *First Concerto* and filled in in the *Second*, here attains a perfection of which I know no other example. (In saying this, I do not think I am being unjust towards the *Concerto* for percussion instruments of Darius Milhaud or the *Ionisation* of Edgar Varèse for two percussion groups, for these two extraordinary exercises in music for massed percussion do not treat the problem within the context of a harmonic mass defined by an ensemble of instruments with fixed tones.)

Xylophones—three timpani (two with pedals)—hanging and fixed cymbals—side-drums with and without snares—bass drum—tom-tom—these were not massed by Bartók as an opposition to the pianos, whatever may have been sometimes said, but to be integrated with them. In fact, what we have here is not a percussion concerto against a harmonic background of chords and counterpoint, but rather an orchestral "tutti", in which every instrument plays its part, in some cases even its thematic part. One must have heard a roll of the bass drum prolonging a low note from the pianos, a trill from the keyboard taken up by the xylophone, to understand the extraordinary novelty of the method, not a fortuitous novelty as in other works, but one pursued with a spirit of logic and invention that gives the measure of Bartók's extraordinary auditory imagination.

M

The general style is basically diatonic, for chromaticism is, as it were, squeezed in between pillars of chords of a fairly orthodox harmony; chromaticism integrates itself into the harmonic background without effort, and from time to time the results have an almost Hindemithian flavour.

The writing for the two pianos has splendid volume, and is based on what is generally called group counterpoint. (Group counterpoint consists of summing-up, in a melodic line carrying synthetic chords, a sequence of harmonies or tightly packed counterpoints, and of making this melodic line evolve contrapuntally at the same time as another melodic line, which itself sums up a sequence of harmonies or tightly-packed counterpoints independent of the first series.)

The key to this co-ordinated movement of two simultaneously present musical masses is the counterpoint of rhythms. It is clear that only a master of rhythm like Bartók could make such a complicated manœuvre effective. He shared this power with three masters still living: Arthur Honneger, Darius Milhaud, and Edgar Varèse (a French composer exiled in the United States through his compatriots' lack of understanding).

It can be seen, then, that the very lavish part played by the percussion instruments in this work has the purpose, in addition to that indicated above, of sustaining and clarifying the base rhythms of each of the two pianos when there is group counterpoint between them.

The *First Movement* of the Sonata shows this technique very characteristically, above all in its expressive prelude which leads into a passage in rapid tempo in which, one by one, all the percussion instruments are integrated. Soon the latter each take over a part of the musical argument from the pianos, thus preparing the hearer for a theme treated in fugue. The dynamic rhythm grows even faster, leading pianos and percussion together into a wild and awe-inspiring dance.

The *Second Movement* is an Andante, in which a very slow, poetic melody is developed with unexpected inflections, irradiated by many little shivers evoked and combined with rare taste from the various percussion instruments.

The *Third Movement*—"Finale Allegro"—is a rondo whose theme, that of an almost mocking dance tune, is expounded first by the xylophone and then taken up by the first piano. The rhythmic and melodic developments shared between the two pianos and the percussion, starting off at a fairly easy pace, become more and more constricted. The more and more closely packed entries lead to such a dynamic tension that one wonders how Bartók is going to resolve it. He does so in masterly fashion, with an airy, relaxed conclusion like the fading of a dream as morning comes.

Even the least musically sophisticated of audiences always give pianists and drummers a frenzied ovation at the end of this extraordinary work; and certainly the performers thoroughly deserve it, for it is an inconceivably difficult work to play.

Bartók later decided to amplify this work to symphonic scale. In 1938 he wrote an orchestral version which is described in the catalogue of his works as *Concerto for Two Pianos and Orchestra*. But at the time of writing, this had not yet been played.

CHAPTER FIVE

SYNTHESIS OF FOLK-LORE ELEMENTS AND CLASSICAL FORM

LIKE THOSE peasants whom Bartók had so often seen on the edge of the fields, contemplating with tranquil satisfaction the vivid patchwork of the harvest crops, Bartók could now look back over the varied field of his labours and find that it was good. He was fifty-seven. It was no longer a time for fresh experiments. Instead, from now on he would concentrate on the cultivation of well-tested personal techniques in the territory he had already conquered. Thus, in his later works, while we shall still admire his strength and elegance, we shall find nothing that is strange. The time had come, in short, for Bartók to reap the fruits of his earlier labours, to classify his methods, and hand them on to posterity.

MIKROKOSMOS

MIKROKOSMOS admirably points the moral. This is, in fact, a collection of a hundred and fifty six piano pieces of graduated difficulty, composed between 1936 and 1937 for Peter Bartók, the composer's second son. Titles like *On the Major Seventh, On the*

Minor Second, show that the composer's primary
intention was to lay for his son the foundations of
a keyboard technique, and to accustom him to the
discontinuous style of modern keyboard fingering.
Thus, *Mikrokosmos* takes its place beside the *Three
Studies* of 1918, which were intended for piano
virtuosos.

Bartók's second purpose, however, was to initiate
his son into the matter of contemporary music. In
Mikrokosmos we find most of our modern problems
in harmony and counterpoint, with Bartók's solutions for them. This side of the work is all the more
valuable because to-day, we tend to become aware
of modern music as a whole through a series of
formulae and experiments, mostly anarchic in
character, and certainly not organized as functions
of the eternal constants of musical expression.

Finally, *Mikrokosmos* contains pieces which are
little masterpieces in their own right. For it is the
gift of genius to confer an unlimited significance
even on didactic works as Couperin, Bach and
Chopin, among many others, have proved. (And
this is a fact which those desirous of restoring music
to its true social function would do well to meditate.)

Furthermore, apart from its moving qualities as
a kind of journal of Bartók's intimate thoughts,
Mikrokosmos offers itself as an excellent tool for the
scholar who wishes to undertake an exegesis on
Bartók's whole development; and in this sense, it
falls into the tradition of *Bagatelles*, *Outdoor
Music* and *Contrasts* (the latter dating from 1938).

CONCERTO FOR VIOLIN AND ORCHESTRA
(1938)

BARTÓK next started upon the composition of one of his most spectacular works: the *Concerto for Violin and Orchestra*, which was completed in December, 1938. The work is in three movements.

The *First Movement*—"Allegro non troppo"— opens with a calm introduction, in which the violin inscribes a rapid and poetic theme which is developed in long lines of equal notes, lines separated from each other by cadences in the Hungarian style. The orchestra finally answers, preparing the entry of the second theme, which is slow, and has a certain flavour of Alban Berg. From then on, the developments of the two themes alternate in a way that suggests a sort of rondo; and this suggestion is further strengthened by the incisive and contradictory clarity of the orchestral *tutti*, at first grave and full when they introduce a version of the first rapid theme, then breathless when they prepare the way for the generous lyricism of the second. The movement ends with a virtuoso cadence: the brusque contrasts between the rapid sections and others dramatically slowed down lead to the re-exposition of the second theme, then to that of the first, and finally, to a series of concluding chords from the violin which are sensationally effective.

The *Second Movement*—"Andante tranquillo"—has a pretty, pastoral line, conveyed in a melody which moves easily and shapes itself happily across decorative developments, certain of which are entrusted to an orchestral palette of an almost impressionist kind, lit up by the meditative celesta. Suddenly, the soloist strikes several chords, then adopts a dramatic, interrupted, chromatic tone, and the whole movement darkens. Finally, after intense trills, hurried passages, a fugitive reappearance of the melody, and a sort of dance movement on three notes, the interrupted musical argument is concluded.

The *Third Movement*, like the first, has two ideas: the first very quick in triple time, the second almost expressionist, with its great leaps that suggest the atonalism of Berg. The two themes are developed in short sections, separated by triumphant ascending motifs above the slow heavy tide of the orchestra with the brass predominating. The work ends in dizzying leaps and bounds sustained by a sequence of chords from the brass which suggest a chorale.

In this composition, one seems to catch at times an echo of Alban Berg's *Concerto for Violin and Orchestra* (1935). But the two works are not really comparable, for the persistence of fundamental rhythms gives to that of Bartók a homogeneity which that of Berg, fine as it is, cannot offer us.

The *Violin Concerto* is dedicated to Zoltán Székely, and it was he who gave the work its first performance in 1939, with the Amsterdam Concertgebouw under the direction of Willem Mengelberg (and not Spivakovsky in the United States during the war, as has often been asserted in the American press).

BARTÓK IN THE EUROPEAN CRISIS

AFTER this work came a period of sterility; it was to endure all through 1938 and a part of 1939. Bartók clearly sensed the impending catastrophe, and the letters which he wrote during his concert tours at this period show the anguish that presentiment brought to his creative spirit. At an international festival in London in June, where he had been invited with his wife to play the *Sonata for Two Pianos and Percussion*, he exclaimed to two of the French participants, "Munich! . . . But don't you see that he (Hitler) plans to devour us all!"

We possess a description by Bartók himself of this state of tragic exasperation—in a letter written to his loyal friend, Madame Müller, on the 13th April, 1938, from Budapest:

"Dear Madame Müller

"Your friendly letter did me a great deal of good. Yes, those were horrible days for us, too. Those days when Austria was attacked. I feel that it is useless to expatiate on this catastrophe—all the more so since you have exactly summed up what we felt ourselves. I should like, however, to add something—the most frightful thing for us at the moment is that we face the threat of seeing Hungary also given over to this régime of bandits and murderers. It is now merely a question of when and how. I cannot imagine how I could live in such a country— or work in such a country, which means the same thing. Strictly speaking, it would be my duty to exile myself, if that is still possible. But even under the most favourable auspices, it would cause me an enormous amount of trouble and moral anguish to earn my daily bread in a foreign country (now at the age of 58, to be forced to take up some hateful task, such as teaching—it is impossible to think of it! in fact, with such a task, I should achieve nothing, for I should not be able to do my really important work). All this adds up to the same old problem, whether to go or stay. And then there is my mother—can I leave her here for ever during the last years of her life?—no, it is impossible.

"What I have been writing now has to do with Hungary where, unfortunately, 'cultured' people, Christians, are almost all submitting themselves to the Nazi régime. Really, I am ashamed to have been born into such a class!

"But I am no less worried when I ask myself—after the destruction of Czechoslovakia and Hungary—when it will be the turn of Switzerland, Belgium, and so on. . . . In fact, what is the situation with you? . . . However good it is now, it always remains possible for a mere thousand men to ask Germany to occupy the country.

"As for my personal situation, at the moment it is rather distressing, for not only has my publisher—Universal Edition—become a Nazi enterprise (the proprietor and the directors have simply been shown the door) but also the A.K.M. (the society that deals with authors' rights—to which both I

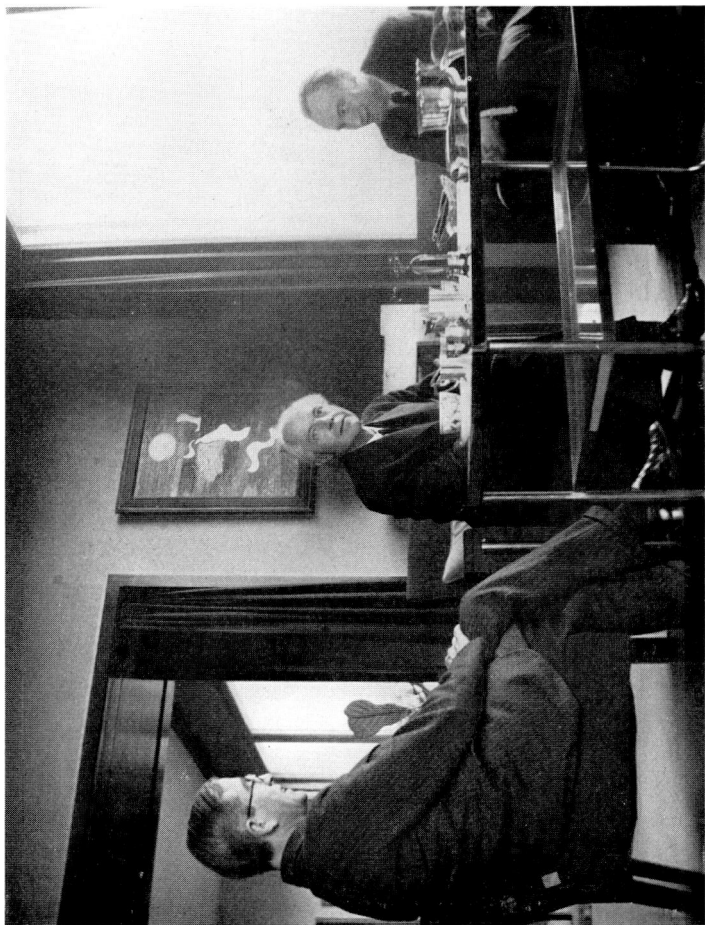

From left to right: Conrad Beck, Béla Bartók, Paul Sachs.

and Kodály belong) is a Viennese society that has just been nazified. In fact, I have just received a scandalous questionnaire about grandparents and other topics, in a word: 'Are you of Germanic race, of similar race, or non-Aryan?' Naturally, neither Kodály nor I have filled in this questionnaire. . . . but really it is a pity that we haven't, because we could have made fun of them, for we should have been able to reply that we are not Aryans—for in fact (as I have learned from the dictionary) 'Aryan' means 'Indo-European': we Hungarians are Finno-Ugrians, and even perhaps northern Turks, and therefore definitely not Indo-Europeans, therefore not Aryans. Another question is: 'Where and when have you been wounded?' Answer: 'Vienna, the 11th, 12th, and 13th of March, 1938!'

"Unhappily, we cannot permit ourselves these jokes. The only thing to do is to ignore these illegal questionnaires and leave them unanswered. The more the A.K.M. launches into illegal questions, the better it is for us, for the more easily we can get out of their clutches; otherwise we should have to remain their prisoners for the next ten years. . . . We have just heard that two great composers' associations of Western Europe would be glad to accept us as members. We must wait and hope for new violations by the A.K.M. of their constitution; then we can do what is necessary. . . .

"The help we have been offered has really touched us. Actually there are three matters about which I should like to ask your help, if that does not cause you too much trouble:

"1.   Since November, I have perceived that Hungary's foreign policy is proceeding on a more and more dubious path.   Since then, I have been wondering how to find a safe place for the manuscripts of my works.   Already I wanted to mention this to you in January, but I did not have the time because of all the work involved in moving house. I am therefore asking you now if you would be kind enough to look after my papers.   Naturally, this would involve no responsibility on your part, I would take all the risk on my own shoulders.   The manuscripts as a whole wouldn't take up very much space—perhaps there is a small trunkful of them.   I should like to send you some of them (perhaps through Stefi Geyer); if I get the chance I shall bring the rest myself.

"2. This has nothing to do with the crisis!   I have lost the copy of the original German translation of my choral works for women's and children's voices.   Perhaps you could ask Herr Huber—is that not the name of your daughters' singing teacher?—to lend you his copy for a short time and have five copies made of it, on the typewriter?   I would send you the money needed through Schulthessen or bring it myself, in June.

"3. A disagreement has cropped up between myself and the Association of German Authors and Composers.   I am sending you, separately, a file on the subject, so you will see what it is all about.   I have also sent my protest to Baden-Baden—where it has been received with surprise, which I regret sincerely, but one can make no exceptions. As you can see on the enclosed programme, they wanted to play the *Five Hungarian Popular Songs*, degraded by a 'transcription', due to an association of composers, the too famous STAGMA. I suppose someone you know, perhaps Paul Sacher, will be present at this music festival. Could you give him these papers to examine and ask him, or anyone else you know who is going to Baden-Baden;

(a) to let me know, after the festival, whether they played my piece even after my protest:

(b) if it is played, to let everybody know that it has been played in spite of my protest;

(c) if the performance does not take place, to find out what reasons are given.

"Do you know that we are going to London in June, where on the 20th we shall play the *Sonata for Two Pianos*. The society is paying a fee of fifty pounds; we are playing the piece first over Radio Luxembourg, so we shall not make a loss on the transaction. On the way back, we should love to pass through Switzerland.

"This letter is very long—forgive me. All our best wishes to you and the Professor. Your friend, Béla Bartók."

DIVERTIMENTO FOR STRING
ORCHESTRA (1939)

THE sterile period came to an end, and from
Bartok's deep inner struggle a masterpiece suddenly
emerged: the *Divertimento for String Orchestra*. The
work is dedicated to Paul Sacher—and no man was
ever more worthy of such a precious tribute than
that great conductor and musical patron. It was, in
fact, due to Sacher that the work first saw the
light. At the beginning of 1939 Bartók and his wife
were deeply depressed at the way events were
shaping. The only thing which could lighten their
mood was a change of country, and with it a radical
change of atmosphere. Paul Sacher understood this,
and persuaded Bartok to take a complete rest,
offering him his chalet at Saanen, in the Gruyère
massif, not far from Fribourg. Bartok found a sort of
enchantment in that noble landscape of pine trees
descending towards the deep crevass through which
the Sarine winds its joyful way. He gave expression
to it in a work of imaginary folk-music, inspired by a
memory of rural festivities. . . .

We find in this work the same quest for orchestral
colour that lends so much beauty to certain passages
of the *Third Quartet*. Only a composer skilled in
handling the very special material of the string
quartet could encompass so many melodies, rhythms,
colours and fancies in the form, approximating to
that of a concerto grosso, of the *Divertimento for
String Orchestra*.

The work is in three parts. The first is a kind of round, evoking the Rumanian "hora", sustained by rapid and re-iterated chords. It is continued by a series of dances in the same psychological atmosphere, interrupted and renewed by brief lyrical incursions intended to pave the way for the pathos of the conclusion.

The andante is a short chromatic recitative undulating through rising shifts of one tone, from double-basses to violins, at each re-exposition. The re-expositions are separated by sharp trills whose colouring suggests the clarinet at the extreme limits of its register, and the tensions thus obtained are most striking.

The finale sets in motion rhythms and a melodic line derived from peasant dances, vibrant with trills, and vigorously supported by cadential unisons. The form is that of a rondo, built around a central episode of an elegiac character. A brief cadence interrupts this episode, and introduces an accelerando rhythm, evoking the swirling peroration of the czardas.

EXILE

THE fateful year 1939 found Bartók in the United States. He had gone there at the invitation of Elizabeth Sprague Coolidge and his old friend Szigeti, who had organized a rather original concert tour for him: Bartók at the piano, Szigeti on the violin, and the jazz celebrity, Benny

Goodman, on the clarinet, interpreting the Master's latest work, *Contrasts*.   In this work—as the title suggests—Bartók wanted to contrast the timbres of the clarinet, now richly smooth, now rasping; those of the violin, now singing, now shrill; and those of the piano, alternately full and dry.

The war thus caught Bartók unprepared, in September, 1939, in New York.   It was difficult to know what to do.   But he decided that, in any case, he would carry out his tour contracts.   During these moments of anguished perplexity, one ray of light shone through: on April 24th, 1940, the League of Composers organized a concert in his honour at the Museum of Modern Art in New York.

In Europe, events were moving fast.   Bartók reached a decision: he wanted to remain in the United States to work for the liberation of Hungary. And that meant going into exile.   It took a great deal of courage to make such a decision, for a man so strongly attached to his local roots.   He returned to Budapest to fetch his wife and his most valuable papers, then set off again.   On October 10th, from the Hôtel des Cornavins in Geneva, he wrote to the faithful and devoted Paul Sacher a short note, "We embark to-morrow—what is to become of us?"

Some days later, he confronted his new destiny, in a country now invaded by the most famous intellectuals and artists of Europe.   There, he was to know discomfort and even acute poverty, since his London publishers, Boosey and Hawkes, and even more his Vienna publishers, Universal Edition, found it legally impossible to send him his royalties which, in any case, at that period, were very meagre. His sources of revenue—a few concerts and the help of devoted friends like Szigeti and Koussevitzky—were sadly intermittent. From Columbia University he received an honorary doctorate, and in February 1941, he gave a course of lectures there. Also, that same year, he was entrusted with the transcription of one of the great collections of Yugoslav music, the Milmann Parry collection. But these activities were more honorific than remunerative. His letters of the period give a clear picture of his difficult situation.

"Concert life here," he wrote on June 20th, "is not exactly attractive: either the impresario is a bad one, or the circumstances are unpropitious—and the war atmosphere will make them even more so in the near future, so that it might almost be better to go back home, whatever the situation is there—that is, even if fascism still reigns. . . ."

In another letter he wrote:

". . . Our situation grows worse from day to day. All I can say is that in the whole of my working life, that is to say for the past twenty years, I have never found myself faced with such a terrible situation as that into which I shall perhaps be plunged in the near future. 'Terrible' is perhaps a little too strong, but not very much so. My wife is bearing up against this heroically, and the worse things go with us, the more energetic, confident and serene she becomes. For example, she is trying to find work

N

as a teacher. But how is she to find pupils, or a post? She asks you for some advice on this matter, if possible. You could perhaps send us the prospectus of the agency with which you negotiated last year. What do you think of it all! For myself, I am becoming rather pessimistic; I have lost all my faith in men and nations, in everything. Unhappily, I have a better knowledge of things than Ditta, so I am perhaps right to be pessimistic. . . .

"We had two pianos free from the Baldwin Piano Company, a baby grand and an upright. I have just heard that they are going to take the upright away. Naturally we haven't got the money to rent a second piano. Thus, we shall no longer be able to practise pieces for two pianos. Every month brings a blow of this sort. I am frantically wondering what will happen next month . . ."

THE SIXTH STRING QUARTET

ON November 3rd, 1940, Bartók gave a two-piano concert with his wife, and then saw no more prospects of concert engagements. He profited by the interval of leisure to revise his *Sixth String Quartet*, the last of his works conceived and elaborated in Hungary.

This work has a dense solidity which defies easy penetration. To understand all its aspects requires more than a careful reading of the score and more than a single hearing of the work—the Gertler

Quartet gave an admirable first performance in Paris in 1946. Yet in spite of its originality, the form of the work is a clearly defined one.

The generative theme is laid bare by the solo viola in a slow and airy introduction. From this theme derives the sonata allegro of the *first movement*. It again introduces, but this time on two instruments, the *second movement*, a march. The *third movement*—"Burletta"—is still preceded by the initial theme, this time on three instruments. The *fourth movement* is the initial theme treated in four parts and developed.

Listening to this quartet, I have often been distracted by the importunate echoes of Beethoven. Again, the content of the very carefully devised musical schema has seemed to me to lack inevitability but possibly this is due to some defect in my own sensibility.

In these last works, I may seem to be abdicating from my task, but that is not the case; this is not the work of a hagiographer, or even of a biographer, but of a respectful and cautious critic. Those who know the enormous proportion of passages of respectable but wearisome failure in the work of even the most undoubted geniuses will approve me when I censure circumspectly the imperfection of certain works of a musician so rich in masterpieces, so full of instruction for his successors, in a word, so considerable as Bartók.

Nor do I hesitate to express certain reservations about the *Concerto for Orchestra* which was commissioned, at the instigation of the ever loyal Szigeti, by Serge Koussevitzky, who conducted its first performance in 1944. Here, however, in strict accuracy, I should make this point: it was only on later reflection that I found it impossible to regard this as a perfect work, not while I was actually listening to it. Even then, however, its inflated orchestration, with the heavy, rich Milhaudian colouring, seemed to my ear to contain elements which I was later unable to reconcile or approve— the embarrassing confusion of styles of succeeding sections.

The general public, on the other hand, which is never worried by a fundamental incoherence if the parts of an incoherent whole are brilliant and picturesque, has always acclaimed this composition, which is indeed full of isolated beauties.

In the *First Movement*—"Andante non troppo" linked to an "Allegro Vivace "(Introduction)—one is fascinated by the diatonic nobility of a theme entrusted to the lower strings which are surrounded by tremors of woodwind and percussion. A flavour of Hindemith insinuates itself into the scoring for the brasses, and particularly into the trombone passages. It is emphasized again when a rapid and tormented theme makes its appearance on the strings, which recalls *The Temptation of St. Anthony*, the third part of Hindemith's symphony *Mathis der Maler*. The third theme recalls the atmosphere of the ancient Magyar cantilenas.

The *Second Movement*—"Allegretto-Scherzando"—

is dominated by a Milhaudian theme carried chiefly by the woodwind above sustained bass rhythms shaped with rich orchestral ornamentation.

The *Third Movement*—"Andante non troppo" (Elegy)—reveals an impassioned theme which, in its many guises, is refracted from all the instrumental levels of the orchestra, thus conveying a shot-silk effect, particularly delightful to the devotees of impressionism.

The *Fourth Movement*—"Allegretto" (Interrupted Intermezzo)—is full of ravishing fantasy and poetry, with just a hint of sarcasm to remind us of Bartók's earlier hunour.

The *Fifth Movement*—"Presto" (Finale)—has a joyous vivacity, expressed through the patterns of Transylvanian dances. Impressive fugato passages prepare the way for a fugue in free form, of which certain episodes lead to an abridged re-entry of the peasant round and a frenzied coda derived from the latter.

SONATA FOR VIOLIN (1949)

IN 1943 Bartók gained a respite from the arduous struggle to earn a living, for to the commission from Koussevitzky was added one from Menuhin for a violin sonata. Bartók finished the work on March 14th, 1944, and Menuhin played it for the first time on the 26th November.

The *First Movement* is a chaconne in G minor, whose expressiveness is emphasized by the contrasts

between the low notes and the planes on which the
tessitura is woven for the instrument (a technique
which Bartók was to use frequently throughout the
work). The development is made up of a system of
very homogeneous variations, punctuated by short
re-entries of the initial theme.

The *Second Movement* is a three-part fugue in C
minor, with an interrupted theme (two quavers,
then three, then four, separated by shorter and
shorter rests); and the breathlessness which we
have noticed several times before in Bartók's
expressive use of thematic material is specially
effective here. A vast central divertimento produces
the same impression of homogeneity as the series of
variations in the first movement.

The *Third Movement* (Melodia) is cunningly written
in a free mode of B-flat, whose chromatic intervals
often recall the tonality of E-flat. Bartók thus links
this movement harmoniously to the first movement
(B-flat having G minor as the relative key) and to
the second (E-flat having C minor as relative key).

The *Fourth Movement* (Presto) stuns the hearer
with its repeated notes played at the tip of the bow;
it evolves round the G minor tonality of the first
movement. This kind of swirling movement round
the same point, the series of augmented seconds, and
the rustic, festive character of the second theme, all
give the movement as a whole the atmosphere of
the Magyar dances. The free rondo form accentuates
this atmosphere.

The style of this work is less strict than in Paul

Hindemith's two sonatas for solo violin, but also less dry, less neo-classical. Bartók must have known these two compositions, for certain modulations achieved by alternating between descending major and minor thirds, very characteristic of Hindemith's style, and found in these two sonatas, are also repeated several times in Bartok's.

VIOLA CONCERTO AND

THIRD CONCERTO FOR PIANO AND

ORCHESTRA

THE year 1944 began for Bartók without too many financial difficulties, but his health was being undermined by a form of anaemia which gradually became pernicious. He was no longer able to undertake concert tours, finding them too exhausting. Those who attended his concerts of January 21st and 22nd, 1943, had applauded the illustrious interpreter-composer for the last time.

Nevertheless, he did not lose heart. At the request of that magnificent viola-player, William Primrose, he began a *Concerto for Viola and Orchestra*. But he had counted too much on his unaided energy; he was unable to orchestrate or complete the work, and he confided his outline plan and finished sketches to the most devoted and learned of his pupils, his compatriot Tibor Serly. The latter achieved a clear and supple orchestration, derived in style and content from the *Third Piano Concerto*.

William Primrose gave the new work its first

performance in the United States in December, 1949, and the first in Europe during the Edinburgh Festival of September 1950. Paris heard it some weeks later under the sparkling direction of Ernest Bour, conducting the Orchestre National. Primrose himself interpreted the work brilliantly, and thus helped to assure its place in the permanent repertory. The English critics were unanimous in their praise for this posthumous score.

The year ended for Bartók among material difficulties of all kinds, and accompanied by a worsening of his illness, which turned into a form of cancer. On top of all, he was torn between joy and anguish at the passage of events. The Nazi hegemony was crumbling; but in its fall it spread ruin and disaster among the cities and capitals of Europe. Budapest was besieged and bombarded, and Bartók did not know whether his friends were alive or dead. Nor did he know what fate had befallen his folk-music recordings, the fruit of so much labour, and not yet transcribed. (In fact, most of them were never found.) Yet Bartók was greatly cheered by several events which occurred in the first half of 1945. First, of course, came the German capitulation, then Bartok's nomination as a member of the new Hungarian parliament, and his restoration to all the official posts from which he had resigned. He seems to have sought to express his new-found joy in the first movement of the *Third Concerto for Piano*, which was started about this time and was dedicated to his wife.

The *First Movement*—"Allegretto"—is in sonata form. Against a tremolo on the strings (similar to the woodwind tremolo at the beginning of *Petrushka*) punctuated by the timpani, there begins on the piano the admirable first theme in E, which extends over a full eighteen bars. Immediately taken up by the orchestra (in G), it then passes by a brusque modulation into D-flat, and then an ascending motif in broken chords is expounded and developed by the piano. A "grazioso" episode in double thirds, first on the piano, then on the woodwind, leads to the second theme, "scherzando", formed of brief syncopated motifs in thirds, cuckoo calls discreetly supported by the percussion, and imitated by the clarinet. The bridge is constructed essentially of materials from the first theme. First the woodwind announces it in A-flat against arpeggios from the piano, which in its turn takes it up again in B-flat in a style very reminiscent of Brahms. The orchestra then interpolates the theme in brief snatches, raising it tone by tone to G sharp. This last note is sustained in trills by the violins, and the re-exposition, completely classical in form, begins.

Second Movement—"Adagio religioso". A short motif formed by the notes of the perfect chord with ornamentations, imitated by the strings, first on C, then on G, E, F, A and finally C again, introduces a piano chorale whose different stanzas are separated by the string motif, and in the harmonic order sketched out in the introduction.

A more animated intermezzo makes its appearance against trills from the strings, and little leaps and staccati from the woodwind. Next, a motif of three notes, taken from the first three notes of the chorale, is heard, then is picked out in the treble of the piano, with a response in pizzicati, and is finally thrown back and forth in every direction, until, augmented by the addition of the xylophone and lastly by the trumpet, it bursts out into a formidable crescendo.

Then the initial chorale reappears, but this time entrusted to the woodwind, while the piano accompanies it a little drily with a two-part counterpoint and with very rapid trills in the caesuras between the stanzas.

The *Third Movement*—"Allegro Vivace"—is in rondo form. Hungarian folk rhythms burst into the principal theme of the finale, in 3/8 time, with the rhythms of quaver-crotchet and crotchet-quaver alternating. A timpani solo leads to the first intermediate "fugato", expounded by the piano, in which the orchestra gradually joins. There is a short recapitulation of the principal theme, then once again the timpani leads into the second, more tranquil interlude in B-flat. Then comes a singing melody from the piano, counterpointed by the strings. As a trio to this interlude, there is another "fugato" on a motif of fifths over which are superimposed the piano scales. There is a recapitulation of the interlude in B-flat, which leads back to the principal theme followed by an extremely brilliant and sonorous stretto (it was again to Tibor Serly that there fell the task of completing the last seventeen bars on the basis of the shorthand sketch of them which Bartók had made).

The *Third Concerto* is one of Bartók's most attractive works, and shows his genius in its most perfect flowering. It is the work of a Master who no longer seeks to set himself problems or, rather, who condenses problems in felicitous formulae, and circumscribes them with a harmonious gesture. It is both "in the tradition" and extremely personal —a synthesis at once of classicism and modernism, of pure music and folk-music. And in spite of difficulties of interpretation in the first movement, with the complexity with which its themes are expounded, and in the rhythmic fantasy of the third, the *Third Concerto* figures very frequently in symphony programmes.

The work was given its first performance in Paris by Madame Valérie Soudère, at the Concerts Pasdeloup conducted by Dervaux, on 29th February, 1948. Some days later, Madame Monique Haas, with the Orchestre National conducted by Roger Désormière, offered a striking interpretation of it to French radio listeners.

Originally conceived for two pianos and orchestra at the request of the famous pianists Bartlett and Robinson, this work in the end had a more moving fate. It became the legacy of the dying Master to the virtuoso who had for so long fought by his side, to that splendid pianist, Ditta Pásztori, his wife.

DEATH (26TH SEPTEMBER, 1945)

THE summer months of 1945, which he had spent with his wife at Lake Saranac, had brought Bartók the solace that only great fighters know before the last battle. He knew, by his increasing weakness, that he was soon to die. A deep serenity took possession of him—a serenity which he expressed in the admirable choral andante of his last concerto, which seems at once a sort of requiem and a farewell to nature.

Back in his little appartment at 309 West Fifty-Seventh Street, Bartók, by the sheer force of his creative power, for a time held at bay the fate seeking to destroy him; above all, he wished to bring his work to an end. Meanwhile, however, his blood-counts showed that almost all hope was gone. He was taken to West Side Hospital. He took with him his rough drafts, and pressed on with his desperate labours. By his bedside, his elder son, Béla, an engineer who had been in America for two years, and his younger son Peter, a volunteer in the United States marines, his wife Ditta Pásztori, and his disciple Tibor Serly, did all they could to help. They prepared the music paper for him, ruled the bar lines, passed the blank sheets to him, while with what strength remained he went on writing. Now only a hundred bars remained to be filled, now only fifty, now twenty, nineteen, eighteen . . . Finally, only seventeen bars were left—those that re-

expound in agogic coda the elements of the first
theme. But that final effort was just beyond his
reach. At dawn on 26th September, Bartok went to
his last rest.

The funeral service took place the following
Friday afternoon at the Universal Funeral Chapel.
It was a sparse congregation—a few friends, com-
patriots, and fellow composers. The only music
played was that of Bach. The burial took place at
Ferncliff Cemetery, Hartsdale.

In his will, Bartók had written:

". . . let my funeral be as simple as possible. If
by chance, after my death, it is purposed to give my
name to a street or erect a monument in a public
square, these are my desires: so long as the squares
in Budapest formerly called Oktagon Square and
Körönd Square bear the names of these men (i.e.
Mussolini and Hitler), and so long as anywhere in
Hungary there is a square or street bearing either of
those names, I do not wish my own name to be
given to any street or square or public monument
throughout the country, nor do I wish that any
commemorative plaque bearing my name be
affixed in any public place.

"This Will has been written entirely in my own
hand and signed by me, and I affirm again that
such are my last wishes."

Bartók's desires have been realized. Throughout
the new Hungary there is not a single street or
square which bears either of those earlier-mentioned
names, synonymous with so much misery. But, on

the other hand, there are many streets and squares—
and even kolkhozes—which bear the name of Béla
Bartók. And that is as it should be; for was he not
himself a builder of bold and robust works, and of
methods effective because founded in the collective
unconscious of a strong, poetic and musical race?

CHAPTER SIX

AN OUTLINE OF THE
ELEMENTS OF BARTOK'S STYLE

I HAVE already noted elsewhere what Bartók the composer owed to Bartók the pianist, and how much the role of the left hand in encompassing different harmonies trained him to a sense of sound volumes and their development. In fact the chord of the fifth is the only sufficiently solid foundation on which to build all the potential superstructures. This impressionist and modal reflex of the pianist's left hand permits an analysis and an easy indentification to be made of all the Bartókian harmonies at their cadential points. It also helps us to grasp the relationships between them (and without relationships between chords, between all the cadential chords, there can be no logic and therefore no harmony; no syntax would be possible between words unlinked by any grammatical relationship; and in music, chords are more or less what verbs, substantives and adjectives are in language, while individual notes are comparable to syllables).

With Bartók, if you look for the fifth formed with the fundamental, and then continue your investigation into all the subsequent chords, you will be able to establish with this succession of fifths a harmonic plane that is striking both for its strictness and simplicity. But we must look at the principles which governed Bartók's use of this "synthesis of fifths".

There is a charming story told of Sviatoslav Prokofiev, the elder of the great Russian composer's two sons. Someone asked him how his famous father set about composing. "First of all," replied the little boy, "Papa writes music like anybody else—then he prokofievizes it!"

So it was with Bartók. He "bartókized" the fifth and the chord it implies according to the laws of acoustics, in other words, he introduced them into a tangible personal universe, declining or conjugating them in his own special fashion.

It was from 1926, from the *Sonata for Piano* onwards, that Bartók's characteristic harmony began to be clearly defined. It is from that period onwards that it is possible therefore to recognize, at the cadential points, the principal harmonies employed by Bartók and to classify them in approximate order. It will at once be noticed that they derive from traditional models for, as we must continually emphasize, Bartók's music is in essence and spirit classical. His language is merely an extension of the syntactical and grammatical possibilities of former Masters: point of departure, cadence, climax, resolution, all are expressed by chords built up on the fifth, by way of modulations with sevenths or dominant ninths, sub-dominant cycles, tonics, all this founded on the clearest insight into the nature and functions of the common chord, major and minor.

But this common chord in its root position is almost the sole basis of modern harmonic volume. We owe it to Bartók that he perceived the vital principle in the harmony of his first model, Richard Strauss, who gained his most brilliant effects by combinations of common chords. (The practice of Florent Schmidt is also extremely interesting in this connection, for with him, the complex chord is not a unity but the superimposition of common chords. In similar fashion, Darius Milhaud's bi-tonality is really founded on two series of common chords evolving separately and simultaneously).

It should also be noted that with Bartók, the chord of the fourth and sixth tends to resume its traditional role. He employed it often as a substratum to his dominant, adding some notes of colour or anticipation. He made skilful use of it for at least twenty years in its strongest tonal form, superimposing the fourth and sixth of the dominant and the fourth and sixth of the sub-dominant, and thus achieved the same effect, but transposed into the tonal feeling, as that of the classical major ninth.

Bartók often uses bi-modality, but it is still his strong feeling for tonality that leads him with such admirable sureness among the reefs of confusion and disorder. The most mistrustful pedant could not mistake the following identities and relationships taken from one of Bartók's piano pieces: C, E-flat, E natural, G-F, F-sharp, A-flat, A natural, C. C being tonic, the first chord is that of the tonic, the

o

second that of the subdominant, and the E-flat
of the first group and the F-sharp and A-flat of the
second group do not alter that fact; on the contrary,
they explain it, since the complex harmonic
aggregation of these two chords evolve towards the
dominant, G, for which the F-sharp and the A-flat
prepare the way.

All Bartók's tonality rests upon rhythm, explicit
and accentuated. For him, as for a classical
musician, the use of the percussion is primarily a
means of articulating the musical argument rather
than, as it often is with the impressionists, a means
of adding orchestral colour. Both secondary
and principal accents are clearly expressed at the
chosen cadential moments.

Since rhythm and metre have a preponderant
place in Bartók's musical inspiration, their formulation through the percussion instruments occurs
frequently and is sometimes almost elevated into a
principle as important as the harmonic principle.
But before embarking on an examination of Bartók's
rhythms, we should observe that they have, particularly on the piano, an influence on the harmonic
representation. Many chords can only be integrated
into a harmonic analysis if one examines the
plasticity and the rhythmical and metrical character
of the melodic phrase that contains them. This is so,
for example, with chords played *martellato*.

In this case, as in the case of clusters of chords,
only the extreme notes are important for harmonic
identification. To take an even better example,

when the rhythm of the cadence is clearly marked, so that there is no possibility of a false metrical interpretation, the composer does not hestiate to free the aggregation built up on the cadential point of balance from servitude to the notes which normally should figure in it.   The chord then acquires a percussive role, and the dominance of rhythm is substituted for the dominance of harmony.

Rhythm! One is forced to refer back to it again and again.   For with a man of such dionysiac temperament as Bartók, rhythm is life itself. Rhythm binds Bartók to his own race, and through rhythm, he is influenced by the confused ferment of songs of labour or festival, by the unconscious suggestion of gesture that arises from daily labour or from the festive dance. . . .

*   *   *

The musical peculiarity of Bartókian rhythm is that it is frequently founded on alternations or combinations of 3/8 and 2/8; 5/8 time is familiar to Bartók, as is also 8/8 time divided into 3/8 plus 2/8 plus 3/8 (a Bulgarian rhythm used only from the *Fifth Quartet* of 1934 onwards), or 1/8 plus 3/8 plus 1/8 plus 3/8.   These divisions, which are peculiar to the Danube Basin, give the music which they underlie a picturesque swing which is wonderfully effective, in essence, they are special forms of the regular metres on which Western music is built, the 5/8 deriving from the 2/4, and the Bartókian 8/8 from the 3/4, these rhythms quite simply having unequal beats in this oriental form. This conception comes from the most distant ages when rhythm was a mixture of shorts and longs. Traces of the mediaeval "perfecta" and "imperfecta" were imported into Bartók's native regions by the European troubadours and the Byzantine singers, and such elements had ancient Greece as their common source, a source still present in certain popular forms.

This interpretation of the 5/8 (one long beat, one short) and of the 8/8 (one long, one short, one long; or one short, one long, one short) is of vital importance in the performance of Bartók's works. The Westerner should never forget this fact, for the effect to be obtained depends on the lightness of the short beat, something like an imperceptible abbreviation. The first quaver of each "rhythmic group" should in general have a primary accent—except, of course, where a different phrasing is specifically indicated.

*   *   *

The melodic lines which Bartók used are extremely varied. After his study of folk melodies, his melodism, at first chromatic and tonal—because romantic in feeling—turned to the diatonic and tended to be based on something other than the tonic, subdominant and dominant. He was attracted to the sixth, third and second, specifically modal. He nevertheless used chromaticism in such a way as to avoid the flabbiness which the modal sections might otherwise have betrayed by comparison with the more tonal modulating sections. Later, after studying the dodecaphonic theory, and adopting a free line which allowed him to use the twelve tones, Bartók nevertheless kept his feeling for the regular scales of seven modal or tonal sounds. And in fact, if we attentively examine his most chromatic texts, we notice that he seems to give the same function to a note whether it is altered by an accidental or not—for instance, an F-sharp in the key of C retains for him four degrees, as if it were an F natural. In short, one might say that the chromatic scale of twelve sounds has for Bartók seven degrees like all the classical scales, but that each of the diatonic degrees of that scale has been divided into two.

The scale that Bartók employs most frequently is that of the mode of F (that is, the key of F without the B-flat of its tonality), with E-flat replacing the leading note. The third F to A is not implacably major, but can be made minor by a flat, and still more frequently, the A natural is present with the A-flat added. A favourite key in which Bartók employs this typical scale is that of C—which gives C, D, E, F-sharp, G, A, B-flat. The C—F-sharp augmented fourth (a tetrachord dear to Debussy) underlines the oriental nature of this scale. The B natural is flattened to destroy its role as the leading note; otherwise, the B natural rising to C would give this scale a strong tonal personality, which would be reinforced by the F-sharp underlining the note G, the dominant of the key of C major.

Thus we find ourselves with a most interesting construction, since it presents a synthesis of the modal and the tonal: the first pentachord C-G is vigorously tonal, while the closing tetrachord C-G is strongly modal, and the F-sharp provides a most effective pivot of modulation. Bartók exploits this dual nature. To do so, he employs methods of scale construction dear to the ancients and to certain mediaeval theorists, superimposing pentachords and tetrachords on their reversed forms or one upon the other, and thus creating new modes. Through these carefully worked out methods, Bartók grasped the secret of how to introduce the chromatic into the modal style, without distorting its nature.

Bartók's treatment of the melodic line also recalls mediaeval disciplines: when the line rises, the degrees of which it makes use are raised by ascending accidentals; when it falls, they are lowered by descending accidentals—in such a way as to underlie the free path left to the melodic pattern, and in spite of the rules for harmonic construction.

*   *   *

This principle of linear evolution dominates all Bartók's use of counterpoint, and must be borne in mind when we seek to understand the movements of his contrapuntal framework within its harmonic universe.

Bartók was encouraged in this bold return to much

earlier laws of counterpoint by his logical sense and his modal background, which fitted him more than any other modern composer to find solutions for the vertical-horizontal complex—solutions which are brilliantly displayed in the *Fifth Quartet*. To be sure, he did not reach this equilibrium without certain aberrations that sometimes bewilder the sympathetic connoisseur who finds himself making a first journey at dizzying speed across landscapes with particularly complicated perspectives—as in the *Third Quartet* for example.

One may gain a better understanding of this special technique from the *Forty-Four Duos* for two violins. This, as I have already mentioned, is a most excellent manual in the art of superimposing melodic lines while preserving the independence of each within their setting.

One particular characteristic of Bartók's counterpoint is his frequent use of the ancient methods of scholastic counterpoint. From time to time, one sees these methods used in modern compositions, but they are generally not the sole element. With Bartók, they are; he has contrapuntal imitations of every kind, that is to say direct, reversed, inverse, crabwise, by contrary movement, etc. Bartók's addiction to these methods may be explained in this way: he was aware that the raw material of sound, which had been liberated by a number of successive revolutions in which the composer himself had played a part, was much too rich—and that it was therefore necessary to limit its use, if one wanted to make a homogeneous work. In short, with such a wealth of material, total liberty might easily lead to anarchy.

This limitation of the material, if it was to be logical, had to be imposed within the principles of melodic super-imposition. Thus one feels in Bartók's work a kind of key plan, which can be set out in this fashion:

Composition for four principal voices:

1. Melodic line;
2. Melodic accompaniment of this line;
3. Metrical line sustaining 1;
4. Varied metrical line (the rhythmic counter-point of 3 which sustains 1).

Bartók's most frequent arrangement of these four elements is: 1 plus 4 plus 2 plus 3.

I must stress, however, that I am concerned here only with a more or less unconscious schema in Bartók's work, in which the different planes are naturally interchangeable.

Bartók's sense of harmony always kept his use of counterpoint very close to the old classical rule—that the universe created by melodic lines in movement should always be capable of integration in a series of chords having a relationship between them. It is true that he drew hitherto unforeseen consequences from this rule; nevertheless, anyone who has made himself familiar with the composer's harmonic vocabulary will easily perceive that he is always at pains to hold the scattered melodic lines round a perceptible tonal centre, to regroup them into fresh tonal masses, in short, to pass them at suitable and pre-established cadential moments through a harmonic filter all of whose elements are in functional relationship with one another.

Between the points of juncture of superimposed melodies, relationships are therefore necessarily established. Here, as in Bartók's use of harmony, we are never confronted with a purely speculative architecture; the experienced pianist always keeps the architect under control. It is true that the scope of certain of the melodic arcs is unusual, and that the general rhythm formed by the colonnade of harmonic pillars is very ample; nevertheless, to the sensitive listener, they have a proper feeling of inevitability.

And this, it must be repeated, is because Bartók feels rhythm in such an "elemental" way; one might almost say that he is aware of the rhythm of a composition before the melodic line. His primal inspiration is a dance, whereas that of his friend Kodály is a song; thus melody for Bartók, being born of rhythmic gesture, remains primarily subject to the laws of metrical and rhythmical development before it is able to impose its own laws of development. This, in fact, is that "thematic rhythm" of which mention has already been made. This way of drawing inspiration from dance and gesture explains the conciseness of Bartók's themes and their brevity, or, when they are more ample in scope, the insistent presence of an underlying metrical element.

It might often be said that for Bartók, melodic

lines and the superimposition of lines are merely a world of volumes in dionysiac evolution. The moulds into which he poured his "divine fury" were theoretically limited in capacity. The sonata, the variation, the rondo—these were all fixed by traditional measurements. In music, however, moulds often go by the board. . . . Each generation breaks them and then refashions others containing a little more than their predecessors. With Bartók, whose inspiration was all fire and flame, the music material boiled up and overflowed all moulds.

When we consider Bartók's work as a whole, there is good reason to assert that the strophic or free forms of folk-poetry and folk-music made a profound impression on the composer. The Beethovenian form raised them to the plane of pure music. As Bartók wrote to von der Null, "In my youth, my ideal of beauty was not so much the manner of Bach or Mozart, as that of Beethoven."

Von der Null elaborates this statement by the composer as follows:

"The study of the piano works shows us how deeply Beethoven was present in the technical reformation of forms accomplished by Bartók. The ternary form of the 'lied' and the 'rondo', as well as the new form of the variation created in the *Improvisations*, are improvements on principles of form which were paramount for Beethoven also. In the place of static forms, in other words, solid and regular forms periodically repeating themselves if possible, Bartók employs the irregular, mobile form which works through the development of its elements. He does for the ternary form of the 'lied' and 'rondo' and for the form of the 'variation' what Beethoven had done for the sonata. This development renders the forms more simple and vital: the elasticity of the ternary form of the 'lied', for example, formerly rigid, now permits the melodic and harmonic forces to evolve as their own energy commands them—they are no longer confined within a formal and inflexible schematic garment."

This continuous development of musical material helped Bartók to discover forms of a powerful dynamic potential.

Bartók is, indeed, as dynamic as a cyclone! The projection of his accelerated movement into the amorphous mass of matter impresses on the latter such gyrations and distortions that only Busoni's expression—"hysteria of form"—is adequate to characterize the relationships between the new forms thus created by the composer and their earlier prototypes.

*   *   *

To conclude this brief technical outline: Bartók's style is the result of an amalgamation of every known method and element in music by one of the most lucid and cultivated minds of the century—a mind gifted with the power of compelling achievement, thanks to the dynamic violence of a restless nature, always avid for liberty. The power of action gave this amalgam its unity, and when the thunders of genius sounded through it, it became a synthesis. In short, Bartók's style is an introduction to the discovery of a universal musical grammar, which the polystylists of contemporary composition have not properly explored.

WORKS BY BARTÓK

Operas and Cantatas

Bluebeard's Castle, one-act opera (1911), op. 11.
Cantata Profana for solo voices, choir, and orchestra (1930).

Ballets

The Wooden Prince (1914), op. 13.
The Wonderful Mandarin (1919), op. 19.

Full Orchestra

Orchestral Scherzo (1903)—unpublished.
Kossuth, a symphonic poem (1903)—unpublished.
Funeral March for Kossuth (1903).
Burlesque (1904), op. 2.
Suite No. 1 (1905), op. 3.
Suite No. 2 (1905–7), op. 4.
Two Portraits (1907–8), op. 5.
Two Images (1910), op. 10.
Four Pieces (1912), op. 12.
Dance Suite (1923).
Rhapsody No. 1 for violin and orchestra (1928).
Rhapsody No. 2 for violin and orchestra (1928).
Music for string instruments, percussion and celesta (1936).
Divertimento (1939).
Orchestral Concerto (1943).

Concertos or Works of Concerto Type

Piano Concerto No. 1 (1926).
Piano Concerto No. 2 (1930–1).
Piano Concerto No. 3 (1945).

Concerto for violin and orchestra (1937–8).
Concerto for two pianos and orchestra (1938–40).
Concerto for viola and orchestra (1945).
Rhapsody for piano and orchestra (1904), op. 1.
Rhapsody No. 1 for violin and orchestra (1928).
Rhapsody No. 2 for violin and orchestra (1928).

Chamber Music

*Quartet (1899)—lost.
First String Quartet (1908).
Second String Quartet (1915–17).
Third String Quartet (1927).
Fourth String Quartet (1928).
Fifth String Quartet (1934).
Sixth String Quartet (1940).
Sonata for two pianos and percussion (1937).
Quintet with piano (1903)—unpublished.
Contrasts for violin, clarinet and piano (1938).
Sonata for violin and piano (1903)—unpublished.
Sonata No. 1 for violin and piano (1921).
Sonata No. 2 for violin and piano (1922).
Violin Sonata, unaccompanied (1943).
Rhapsody No. 1 for violin and piano (1928).
Rhapsody No. 2 for violin and piano (1928).
Rhapsody for violoncello and piano (1928).
Forty-Four Duos for two violins (1931).

Piano

*The Course of the Danube (1890)—lost.
Scherzo (1897)—unpublished.
Spring Song (1897)—unpublished.
Waltz (1897)—unpublished.
Three Piano Pieces (1897)—unpublished.
Piano Sonata (1898).
Burlesques (1902).
*Pieces for piano (1903)—lost?

Sonata Movement for Left Hand (1903).
Four Fragments (1903).
Fourteen Bagatelles (1908), op. 6.
Ten Easy Pieces (1908).
Two Elegies (1908–1910), op. 8.
For Children (eighty-five pieces) (1908–9).
Three Burlesques (1908–10), op. 8 c.
Sketches (1908–10), op. 9.
Four Funeral Chants (1910).
Allegro Barbaro (1911).
Eighteen Pieces for Beginners at the piano (1913).
Sonatina (1915).
Suite (1916).
Three Studies (1918), op. 18.
Improvisations (1920), op. 20.
Sonata (1926).
Out Doors (1926)—five pieces.
Nine Little Pieces (1926).
Three Rondos (1916–27).
Little Suite (1936).
Mikrokosmos (1936–7).
For transcriptions and harmonizations, see *Folk Music*.

Melodies

Three melodies for voice and piano accompaniment (1898).
Four melodies for voice and piano (1902).
Five melodies for voice and piano on poems by Ady (1916),
    op. 16.

Folk Songs

Four Songs (1904).
Twenty Popular Hungarian Songs, in collaboration with
    Kodaly (1906).
Eight Popular Hungarian Melodies for voice and piano
    (1907–17).
Five Village Scenes for voice and piano (1924).
Twenty Popular Songs for voice and piano (1929).

For Choirs without Accompaniment

Popular Hungarian Songs for male choirs (1912).
Popular Hungarian Songs for mixed choirs (1930–1).
Székely Songs for male choirs (1932).
Popular Hungarian Songs for choirs (1935).
Twenty-seven two- and three-part Choral Pieces for women's and children's choirs (1935).
Three Choral Pieces in three voices for male choirs (1935).

Choirs and Piano

Four Slovak Popular Songs (1917).
Popular Songs for male voices (1917).

Instrumental Folk Music for Piano

Three Hungarian Popular Songs (1907).
Two Rumanian Dances for piano (1909–10).
Fifteen Hungarian Peasant Songs for piano (1914–17).
Popular Rumanian Dances for piano (1915).
Rumanian Christmas Songs ("Colindas") (1915).

Violin and Piano

Hungarian Popular Songs, transcription by Szigeti.
Four Popular Rumanian Dances for violin (1917) transcription by Székely.

Orchestral Folk Music

Popular Rumanian Dances for chamber orchestra (1917).
Transylvanian Dances for full orchestra (1931).
Hungarian Peasant Songs for orchestra (1933).

Voice and Orchestra

Five Village Scenes for mezzo-soprano and orchestra (1926).
Hungarian Peasant Songs for voice and orchestra (1933).

A SELECTED BIBLIOGRAPHY

Books by Béla Bartók

Hungarian: *Magyar Népdálok* (with Zoltán Kodály), Budapest 1906.
Erdelyi Székely Népdálok (with Zoltán Kodály), A collection of 150 Transylvanian songs, Budapest 1923.
A Mágyar Népdal: 320 Melodies. Budapest 1924.
Népzenénk és a Szomszéd Népek Nepzenéje: 127 Melodies. Budapest 1934.
Miért es Hogyan Gyüjtsünk Népzenét, (Why and how we collect Folk Music) Budapest 1936.

Rumanian: *Cântece poporale românesti din Comitatul Bihar* (Popular Songs from the Bihar County). This is the first important collection of folk tunes published by Bartók. It includes 371 melodies and obtained the greatest prize offered by the Rumanian Academy. Bucharest 1913.
Scrieri Marunte despre muzica populara româneasca. Bucharest 1937.

German: *Die Volksmusik der Rumänen von Maramures,* 365 Melodies. München 1923.
Das Ungarische Volkslied. Berlin 1925.
26.000 Slowakische Volkslieder. Slovenska Matica 1928-1929.
Die Melodien der Rumänischen Colinde (Christmas Carols). 484 Melodies. Vienna 1935.

French: *Pourquoi et comment recueille-on la musique populaire?* Geneva 1948.

P

English: *Hungarian Folk Music.* Translated from the German by M. D. Calvocoressi, Oxford University Press, London 1931.

Articles by Béla Bartók (in English and French)

"La musique populaire hongroise." *La revue musicale*, Paris 1920.

"Kodaly's Trio." *Musical Courier*, U.S.A. 1920.

"The relation of folk-song to the development of the music of our time." *The Sackbut*, London 1921.

"The folk songs of Hungary." *Pro Musica*, New York 1928.

"The national temperament in music." *Musical Times*, London 1929.

"The peasant music of Hungary." *Musical Courier*, U.S.A. 1931.

"Hungarian peasant music." *Musical Quarterly*, U.S.A. 1933.

"The Liszt Problem." *Monthly Musical Courier*, London 1949.

"Parry Collection of Yugoslav Folk Music." *The New York Times* 1942.

"Folksong Research in Eastern Europe." *Musical America*, New York 1943.

"Race Purity in Music." *Tempo*, London 1944.

"Some linguistic observations." *Tempo*, London 1946.

N.B.   Béla Bartók's unpublished researches, notes, and studies in folk music are deposited with Dr. George Herzog of the Department of Anthropology, Indiana University, U.S.A.

Important Books and Articles on Béla Bartók

Abraham, Gerald: "The Bartók of the Quartets." *Music and Letters*, London, October 1945.

Bekker, Paul: *Béla Bartók.* (Klang and Eros), Vienna 1922.

Blom, Eric: *Stepchildren of Music.* London 1926.

Casella, Alfredo: *In memoria di Béla Bartók.* Rome 1947.

Dent, Edward J: "A Hungarian Bluebeard." *The Nation and The Athenaeum*, June 1923.

Ewen, David — *The Book of Modern Composers.* (Knopf), New York 1942

Gray, Cecil: *A Survey of Contemporary Music.* (Oxford University Press), 1924 and 1927.

Haraszti, Emil: *Béla Bartók: His life and works.* (Lyrebird Press), Paris 1933.

Heseltine, Philip: "Modern Hungarian Composers". *Musical Times*, London 1922.

Kodály, Zoltán: "Béla Bartók." *La revue musicale*, Paris 1921.

Rostand, Claude: "Béla Bartók: chemins et contrastes du musicien." *Contrepoints*, April 1946.

Stevens, Halsey: *The Life and Music of Béla Bartók.* (Oxford University Press), 1953.

Szigeti, Joseph: *With Strings Attached.* (Cassell), London 1949.

Tharaud, Jean et Jérome: *La musique contemporaine de Hongrie*, Paris 1943.

Vlad, Roman: "Béla Bartók: Musica e tempo." *Il Ponte*, Feb. 1947.

RECORDS OF BARTÓK'S WORKS

AVAILABLE IN ENGLAND AND AMERICA

Orchestral Works

Piano Concerto No. 2 (1931)
 Andor Földes and Lamoureux Orch./Bigot. American Vox
 PLP 6620, LP, U.K.[1]; Polydor 566320–2, France.

Piano Concerto No. 3 (1945)
 György Sándor and Philadelphia/Ormandy. Columbia
 LX 1271–3; Auto Columbia LX 8710–12; American
 Columbia D 12537–9; Music Library ML 4239 LP.

Concerto for Violin and Orchestra (1938)
 Menuhin and Dallas Symph. Orch./Dorati. HMV DB
 6361–5, U.K.; Auto HMV DB 9291–5, U.K.; Victor
 11–9552/6 set M 1120.
 M. Rostal and L.S.O./Sargent. Decca X 23104; American
 Decca LXT 2574 and LON LLP 302, both LP, both
 U.K., U.S.A. and Europe.

Concerto for Orchestra (1943)
 Amsterdam Concertgebouw/Van Beinum. Decca AK
 2042–6, U.K. and Europe; Decca LXT 2529, U.K. and
 Europe; American Decca EDA 105; American Decca
 LON LA 91; American Decca LLP 5, U.S.A.
 Pittsburgh Symph./Reiner. American Columbia 12918–
 23 D; Music Library ML 4102 LP.
 Budapest Phil./Kórodi. Supraphon Sup 19050–5; Ultraphon
 U.G. 23276–81.

---

[1] Where name of country is stated, the record is known to be available in
that country.

Music for Strings, Percussion and Celesta (1936)
Los Angeles Chamber Symph./Byrns. Decca Capitol CK
51001–3, U.S.A.; Decca Capitol CCL 7500, Europe and
U.K.

Philharmonia/Karajan. Columbia LX 1371–4.

Two Portraits, Op. 5 (1908)
New Symph. Orch./Autori. Bartók Recording Studios
BRS 303, LP, U.S.A.

Rhapsody Op. 1, *Piano and Orchestra* (1904)
Andor Földes and Lamoureux Orch./Desormière. Polydor A
6339–40

Suite Op. 4, *Orchestra*
Symph. Orch./Swoboda. Concert Hall Society CHS Set D4;
Concert Hall Society CHS Set DL 4, LP.

Dance Suite (1923)
New Symph. Orch./Autori. Bartók Recording Studios BRS
302, LP, U.S.A.

Divertimento for Strings (1939)
String Orch./Serly. Bartók Recording Studios BRS 905,
LP, U.S.A.
Samaran-Taffanel Ensemble. Selmer LPG 8005, LP.

Two Images, Op. 10 (1910)
New Symph. Orch./Serly. Bartók Recording Studios BRS
305, LP, U.S.A.

The Miraculous Mandarin, Ballet (1919) *Orchestral Suite*
New Symph. Orch./Serly. Bartók Recording Studios BRS
301, LP, U.S.A.

Dance Suite, Two Portraits
New Symph. Orch./Autori. Bartók Recording Studios BRS
304, LP, U.S.A.

Chamber Music

Quartets, String
Collection played by the Juilliard Quartet
No. 1 *A minor.* American Columbia Set MM 882;
American Columbia ML 4278, LP.

No. 2 A minor. American Columbia Set MM 883; American Columbia ML 4278, LP.

No. 3 (1927). American Columbia Set MX 331; American Columbia ML 4279, LP.

No. 4 (1928). American Columbia Set MM 884; American Columbia ML 4279, LP.

No. 5 (1934). American Columbia Set MM 885; American Columbia ML 4280, LP.

No. 6 (1939). American Columbia Set MM 883; American Columbia ML 4280, LP.

No. 1 A Minor
Pro Arte Quartet. Victor 8842–5.

No. 2 A minor
Budapest Quartet. HMV DB 2842–5; Victor 14123–6.

No. 3
New Music Quartet. Bartók Recording Studios BRS 901, LP, U.S.A.

No. 4
Guilet Quartet. Concert Hall Society CHS Set A8.

No. 5
Hungarian Quartet. HMV C 3511–4.

No. 6
Hungarian Quartet. HMV DB 9389–92, Auto, U.K.; HMV DB 6896–9.
Gertler Quartet. Decca K 1433–6; American Decca Set EDA 73.
Erling Block Quartet. HMV DB 20104–66, U.K.

Forty-four Duets for Two Violins (1938)
G. Lengyel and A. M. Gründer. Selmer Y 8013/20.
V. Aitay and M. Kuttner. Bartók Recording Studios BRS 907, LP, U.S.A.; Period SPLP 506; (Period issued as Nixa in U.K.)

Contrasts, Violin, Clarinet and Piano (1938)
J. Szigeti, B. Goodman, B. Bartók. Columbia C LOX 485–6; American Columbia 70362/3D.

R. Mann, S. Drucker, L. Hambro.   Bartók Recording
Studios BRS 916, LP, U.S.A

Two Rhapsodies, Violin or Violoncello and Piano, No. 1 (1928)
J. Starker, violoncello, O. Herz.   Program EXLP 702;
Nixa EXLP 702.
J. Szigeti and B. Bartók.   Columbia LOX 519; American
Columbia 11410 D.

Sonatas, Violin and Piano
No. 1 (1921)
Menuhin and A. Baller.   Victor 12–0748/51; Victor LM
1009, LP.
I. Stern and A. Zakin.   American Columbia ML 4376, LP.
No. 2 (1922)
T. Spivakovsky and A. Balsam.   Concert Hall Society
Set AA; Concert Hall Society CHS 39, LP.

Viola Concerto
William Primrose, viola; New Symph. Orch./Serly and
Autori.   Bartók Recording Studios BRS 309, LP, U.S.A.

Two Rhapsodies, Violin and Orchestra
Vardi violin, New Symph. Orch./Serly and Autori.   Bartók
Recording Studios BRS 306, LP, U.S.A.

Sonata for Solo Violin (1944)
Menuhin.   HMV DB 9231–3; U.K.; Victor 12–1082/4 Set
DM 1350; Victor LM 1078, LP.

Sonata, Two Pianos and Percussion (1938)
B. and D. P. Bartók, H. Baker and E. Rubsän.   American
Vox PL 6010, LP, U.S.A.
B. and D. P. Bartók and percussion.   Classic C 2113/5.
W. Masselos, M. Ajemian; S. Goodman and A. Marcus
Dial 1; Magic Tone Records CL 1 LP.
G. Gorini, S. Lorenzi; Stabile Fiorentino Orch. and per-
cussion/Gracis.   Durium SA 101/3; Pacific 6506/8.

Piano
Allegro Barbaro (1911)
B. Bartók.   Bartók Recording Studios BRS 903, LP, U.S.A.

H. Leygraf. HMV X 7330, U.K.
Farnadi. Columbia GFX 148.

Fourteen Bagatelles, Op. 6 (1908)
No. 2
  B. Bartók. Bartók Recording Studios BRS 903, LP, U.S.A.

Three Burlesques, Op. 8c (1908–11)
  No. 1 Quarrel, *No.* 2 A bit drunk
    E. Kilényi. American Columbia 70348 D.
  No. 2 only
    B. Bartók. Bartók Recording Studios BRS 903, LP, U.S.A.
  Arranged for Orchestra
    Budapest Symph./Komor. HMV HUC 110.

Four Dirges (1910)
No. 2 Arranged for Orchestra
  Budapest Symph./Komor. HMV HUC 110.

Ten Easy Pieces (1908)
  No. 5 Evening in Transylvania, *No.* 10 Bear Dance
    B. Bartók. American Vox 650, U.S.A.; American Vox
    PLP 6010, LP, U.S.A.; Classic C 2075/6.

  Arranged for Band
    2nd Infantry Regiment. HMV AM 3215.

For Children (1909)
  Vol. 1 Nos. 3, 4, 6, 10, 12, 13, 15, 18, 19, 21, 26, 30, 31, 34, 35
    B. Bartók. American Vox 650/1, U.S.A.; American Vox
    PLP 6010, LP, U.S.A.

  Vol. 1 Nos. 1, 3, 5, 7, 10, 13, 16, 22, 30, 31. *Vol.* 2 Nos. 2, 14, 15
    31
    G. Moore. HMV B 9882, U.K.

  Vol. 1 Nos. 22, 31, 30, 40
    L. Kentner. Columbia DX 989.

  Vol. 1 Nos. 6, 13, 18, 25, 31, 36, 40
    Arranged for violin and piano by Szigeti: "Hungarian
    Folktunes".
    I. Haendel and I. Newton. Decca K 2029, Europe and U.K.
    E. and A. Wolf. Tono A 150.

Vol. 11 *No.* 8, Dance
    Victor Orchestra. Victor 45–5039.

Fifteen Hungarian Peasant Songs, piano (1914–17)
    Andor Földes. American Vox PLP 6410, LP, U.SA

    Nos. 7–12, 14, 15
        B. Bartók. Pacific 6501; Patria MRE 63.

Out Doors suite (1926)
    L. Hambro (improvisations) Bartók Recording Studios
    BRS 902, LP, U.S.A.
    J. Germain. Classic C 2044/6.

Petite Suite (1938)
    (from Duos for Two Violins, Nos. 28, 32, 38, 43, 16, 36)
        B. Bartók. Continental 4005; Remington LP, U.S.A.

    No. 5 Bagpipes only
        B. Bartók. Pacific 5010.

Three Rondos on Folktunes (1916–17)
    Lily Kraus. Parlophone PXO 1025/6.

    No. 1 only
        B. Bartók. Continental 4006; Remington LP, U.S.A.;
        Pacific 5010.
        P. Solymos. Elite 7052.
        H. Leygraf. HMV X 7330, U.K.
        M. Ajemian. Victor 12–0343.

Rumanian Christmas Carols (1915)
    Series 1, Nos. 2, 5. Series 2, No. 9.
    G. Moore. HMV B 9883, U.K.

Two Rumanian Dances, *Op.* 8a (1910)
    No. 1 only
        B. Bartók. Bartók Recording Studios. BRS 903, LP,
    U.S.A.
        P. Solymos. Elite 7052.

Six Rumanian Folk-dances (1915)
    Lily Kraus (Rondo No. 3). Parlophone PXO 1026.
    Kollersgorskaya. U.S.S.R. 14653/4.

Arranged for Violin and Piano by Székely
Menuhin and Marcel Gazelle.   HMV DB 6178, U.K.;
    Victor 12–1061.
  I. Haendel and I. Newton.   Decca K 1837, Europe and
    U.K.; American Decca LON T 5409.
  B. Gimpel and A. Balsam.   American Vox Set 616.
  A. Garami and G. Solocsány.   Pacific PI 1574.
  L. Gilels and A. Makarov.   Ultraphon B 15038.
  D. Zsigmondy and A. Nissen.   Polydor 62871.

Nos. 1–4, and 6 only
  Z. Székely and G. Frid.   Decca K 872.

Nos. 1, 3, 4, 6 only
  T. Spivakovsky and A. Balsam.   Concert Hall Society
    CHS Set AA; Concert Hall Society CHC 39, LP.

Nos. 1, 5, 6 only
  D. Erlih and M. Bureau.   HMV DA 5041, France.

Arranged for Orchestra by Bartók (1917)
  Residente/Schuurman.   Decca X 10038.
  Columbus Phil./I. Solomon.   Discovery DL 4004, LP.

Arranged for String Orchestra by Willner
  Stuyvesant Sinfonietta/Shulman. American Columbia ML
    2121, LP.
  Philharmonia/Lambert.   Columbia DX 1221.

Sonata (1926)
  Andor Földes.   Polydor 566318/9; American Vox PL
    6620, LP, U.K.

Sonatina (1915)
  B. Bartók.   Bartók Recording Studios BRS 003, LP, U.S.A.
  M. Barzetti.   HMV S 10491.
  J. Germain.   Classic C 2020.

Three Hungarian Folk-tunes (from Album dedicated to Paderewski)
  B. Bartók.   Continental C. 1193; Remington, LP, U.S.A.

Eight Improvisations on Hungarian Folk-songs, Op. 20 (1920)
  L. Hambro. Bartók Recording Studios BRS 902, LP, U.S.A.

Nos. 1, 2, 6, 7, 8
   B. Bartók. Continental C 4007; Remington, LP, U.S.A.

Nine Little Pieces (1926)

No. 6 Song, *No.* 8 Tambourin
   B. Bartók. Continental C 1193; Remington, LP, U.S.A.;
   Pacific 5010; Patria MR 64.

No. 9 Preludio all'ungherese
   B. Bartók. Continental 4006; Remington, LP, U.S.A.

Mikrokosmos (153 pieces) (1926–37)

Nos. 94, 100, 108, 109, 113, 120, 128, 129, 131, 133, 138, 140,
   142, 148–153
   B. Bartók. American Columbia 71112/4D.

Nos. 124, 146, (*a*) Staccato, (*b*) Ostinato
   B. Bartók. Columbia DB 1790; American Columbia DB
   1306.

Nos. 109, 113, 128, 142
   E. Farnadi. Columbia DB 1790.

Nos. 142, 146
   Andor Földes. Polydor 566319.

No. 148
   M. Ajemian. Victor 12–0343.

Nos. 69, 127, 145 Arranged for Two Pianos by Bartók
   B. and D. P. Bartók. Continental 4008; Remington, LP,
   U.S.A.

Nos. 102, 108, 116, 139, 142 arranged for String Quartet by
   Serly
   New Music Quartet. Bartók Recording Studios BRS 901,
   LP, U.S.A.

Nos. 102, 117, 137, 139, 142, 151, 153 arranged for Orchestra
   by Serly (1942)
   New Symph. Orch./Serly. Bartók Recording Studios BRS
   303, LP, U.S.A.

Nos. 97, 128, 113, 125, 130
   G. Moore. HMV B 10409, U.K.

Nos. 138, 100, 139, 116, 109 135, 139
   G. Moore. HMV B 10410, U.K.

Prelude from Homage to Paderewski, arranged for Orchestra by
   Serly
   New Symphony Orchestra/Serly.   Bartók Recording
   Studios BRS 303, LP, U.S.A.

Three Rondos, Sonatina, Eight Pieces for Children
   Ilona Kabos.   Bartók Recording Studios BRS 917, LP,
   U.S.A.

Vocal

Enchanting Song (No. 14 of twenty-seven part songs, 1935)
   Morriston Boys Choir/Syms. Decca 1157, Europe and U.K.

Twenty Hungarian Folk-songs (1906) two only. *Twenty Hungarian*
   Folk-songs (1929) four only
   L. Chabay tenor, T. Kozma piano.   Bartók Recording
   Studios BRS 904, LP, U.S.A.

Eight Hungarian Folk-songs (1907–17)
   L. Chabay tenor, T. Kozma piano.   Bartók Recording
   Studios BRS 904, LP, U.S.A.
   N. Valery soprano, R. Goehr piano. Allegro AL 106, LP.

 Nos. 1, 2, 3, 4, only
   M. Laszlo soprano, G. Favaretto piano. Parlophone AT
   0155.

Slovak Songs (1914–18)
   Slovak Teachers Chorus/Strelac. Esta Z 27082.

Ten Hungarian Folk-songs (1906, revised 1938)
  Nos. 1, 2, 3, 8, 10, only
   J. Boráros baritone, Németh-Sanorinsky piano. Ultraphon
   C 23572.

Hungarian Folk-songs Vol. 11
   L. Chabay tenor, T. Kozma piano.   Bartók Recording
   Studios BRS 914, LP, U.S.A.

APPENDIX

I. THE INFLUENCE OF PEASANT MUSIC ON MODERN MUSIC

At the beginning of the twentieth century there was a turning point in the history of modern music. The excesses of the romanticists began to be unbearable for many. There were composers who felt: "this road does not lead us anywhere; there is no other solution but a complete break with the nineteenth century".

Invaluable help was given to this change (or let us rather call it rejuvenation) by a kind of peasant music unknown up till then.

The right type of peasant music is most varied and perfect in its forms. Its expressive power is amazing, and at the same time it is void of all sentimentality and super-fluous ornaments. It is simple, sometimes primitive, but never silly. It is the ideal starting point for a musical renaissance, and a composer in search of new ways cannot be led by a better master. What is the best way for a composer to reap the full benefits of his studies in peasant music? It is to assimilate the idiom of peasant music so completely that he is able to forget all about it and use it as his musical mother-tongue.

In order to achieve this, Hungarian composers went into the country and made their collections there. It may be that the Russian Stravinsky and the Spaniard Falla did not go on journeys of collection, and mainly drew their material from the collections of others, but they too, I feel sure, must have studied not only books and museums but the living music of their countries.

In my opinion, the effects of peasant music cannot be deep and permanent unless this music is studied in the country as part of a life shared with the peasants. It is not enough to study it as it is stored up in museums. It is the character of peasant music, indescribable in words, that must find its way into our music. It must be pervaded by the very atmosphere of peasant culture. Peasant motifs (or imitations of such motifs) will only lend our music some new ornaments: nothing more.

Some twenty to twenty-five years ago well disposed people often marvelled at our enthusiasm. How was it possible, they asked, that trained musicians, fit to give concerts, took upon themselves the "subaltern" task of going into the country and studying the music of the people on the spot? What a pity, they said, that this task was not carried out by people unsuitable for a higher type of musical work. Many thought our perseverance in our work was due to some crazy idea that had got hold of us.

Little did they know how much this work meant to us. We went into the country and obtained first-hand knowledge of a music that opened up new ways to us.

The question is, what are the ways in which peasant music is taken over and becomes transmuted into modern music?

We may, for instance, take over a peasant melody unchanged or only slightly varied, write an accompaniment to it and possibly some opening and concluding phrases. This kind of work would show a certain analogy with Bach's treatment of chorales.

Two main types can be distinguished among works of this character.

In the one case accompaniment, introductory and concluding phrases, are of secondary importance, they only serve as an ornamental setting for the precious stone: the peasant melody.

It is the other way round in the second case: the melody only serves as a "motto" while that which is built round it is of real importance.

All shades of transition are possible between these two extremes and sometimes it is not even possible to decide which of the elements is predominant in any given case. But in every case it is of the greatest importance that the musical qualities of the setting should be derived from the musical qualities of the melody, from such characteristics as are contained in it openly or covertly, so that melody and all additions create the impression of complete unity.

At this point I have to mention a strange notion widespread some thirty or forty years ago. Most trained and good musicians then believed that only simple harmonizations were well suited to folk-tunes. And even worse, by simple harmonies they meant a succession of triads of tonic, dominant and possibly subdominant.

How can we account for this strange belief? What kind of folk-songs did these musicians know? Mostly new German and Western songs and so-called folk-songs made up by popular composers. The melody of such songs usually moves along the triad of tonic and dominant; the main melody consists of a breaking up of these chords into single notes ("Oh Du lieber Augustin"). It is obvious that melodies of this description do not go well with a more complex harmonization.

But our musicians wanted to apply the theory derived

from this type of songs to an entirely different type of Hungarian songs built up on "pentatonic" scales.

It may sound odd, but I do not hesitate to say: the simpler the melody the more complex and strange may be the harmonization and accompaniment that go well with it. Let us, for instance, take a melody that moves on two successive notes only (there are many such melodies in Arab peasant music). It is obvious that we are much freer in the invention of an accompaniment than in the case of a melody of a more complex character. These primitive melodies moreover, show no trace of the stereotyped joining of triads. That again means greater freedom for us in the treatment of the melody. It allows us to bring out the melody most clearly by building round it harmonies of the widest range varying along different keynotes. I might also say that the traces of polytonality in modern Hungarian music and in Stravinsky's music are to be explained by this possibility.

Similarly, the strange turnings of melodies in our Eastern European peasant music showed us new ways of harmonization. For instance the new chord of the seventh which we use as a concord may be traced back to the fact that in our folk melodies of a pentatonic character the seventh appears as an interval of equal importance with the third and the fifth. We so often heard these intervals as of equal value in the succession, that what was more natural than that we should try to make them sound of equal importance when used simultaneously? We sounded the four notes together in a setting which made us feel it not necessary to break them up. In other words: the four notes were made to form a concord.

The frequent use of quart intervals in our old melodies suggested to us the use of quart chords. Here again what

Q

we heard in succession we tried to build up in a simul-
taneous chord.

Another method by which peasant music becomes
transmuted into modern music is the following: The composer does not make use of a real peasant melody but
invents his own imitation of such melodies. There is no
true difference between this method and the one described
above.

Stravinsky never mentions the sources of his themes.
Neither in his titles nor in footnotes does he ever allude
to it, whether a theme of his is his own invention or whether
it is taken over from folk-music. In the same way the old
composers never gave any data: let me simply mention
the beginning of the *Pastoral Symphony*. Stravinsky
apparently takes this course deliberately. He wants to
demonstrate that it does not matter a jot whether a
composer invents his own themes or takes his themes from
elsewhere. He has a right to use musical material taken
from all sources. What he has judged suitable for his
purpose has become through this very use his mental
property. In the same manner Molière is reported to have
replied to a charge of plagiarism: "Je prends mon bien
où je le trouve". In maintaining that the question of the
origin of a theme is completely unimportant from the
artist's point of view, Stravinsky is right. The question
of origins can only be interesting from the point of view of
musical documentation.

Lacking any data I am unable to tell which themes of
Stravinsky's at his so-called "Russian period" are his
own inventions and which are borrowed from folk-
music. This much is certain, that if among Stravinsky's
thematic material there are some of his own invention
(and who can doubt that there are) these are the most
faithful and clever imitations of folk-songs. It is also

notable that during his "Russian" period, from *Le Sacre du Printemps* onward, he seldom uses melodies of a closed form consisting of three or four lines, but short motifs of two or three bars and repeats them "a la ostinato". These short recurring primitive motifs are very characteristic of Russian music of a certain category. This type of constructions occurs in some of our old music for wind instruments and also in Arab peasant dances.

This primitive construction of the thematic material may partly account for the strange mosaic-like character of Stravinsky's work during his early period.

The steady repetition of primitive motifs creates an air of strange feverish excitement even in the sort of folk-music where it occurs. The effect is increased a hundred-fold if a master of Stravinsky's supreme skill and his precise knowledge of dynamic effects employs these rapidly chasing sets of motifs.

There is yet a third way in which the influence of peasant music can be traced in a composer's work: neither peasant melodies nor imitations of peasant melodies can be found in his music, but it is pervaded by the atmosphere of peasant music. In this case we may say, he has completely absorbed the idiom of peasant music which has become his musical mother-tongue. He masters it as completely as a poet masters his mother-tongue.

In Hungarian music the best example of this kind can be found in Kodály's work. It is enough to mention *Psalmus Hungaricus*, which would not have been written without Hungarian peasant music. (Neither of course, would it have been written without Kodály.)

*   *   *

Many people think it a comparatively easy task to write a composition round folk-tunes—a lesser achievement at least than a composition on "original" themes—because, they think, the composer is dispensed of part of the work: invention of themes.

This way of thought is completely erroneous. To handle folk-tunes is one of the most difficult tasks; equally difficult if not more so than to write a major original composition. If we keep in mind that borrowing a tune means being bound by its individual peculiarity we shall understand one part of the difficulty. Another is created by the special character of a folk-tune. We must penetrate into it, feel it, and bring it out in sharp contours by the appropriate setting. The composition round a folk-tune must be done in a "propitious hour" or—as is generally said—it must be a work of inspiration just as much as any other composition.

There are many who think the basing of modern music on folk-music harmful and not suited to our time.

Before arguing with that school of thought let us consider how it is possible to reconcile music based on folk-music with the modern movement into atonality, or music on twelve tones.

Let us say frankly that this is not possible. Why not? Because folk-tunes are always tonal. Folk-music of atonality is completely inconceivable. Consequently, music on twelve tones cannot be based on folk-music.

The fact that some twentieth-century composers went back for inspiration to old folk-music acted as an impediment to the development of twelve-tone music.

Far be it from me to maintain that to base his music on folk-music is the only way to salvation for a composer in our days. But I wish that our opponents had an equally liberal opinion of the significance of folk-music.

It is only recently that one of our reputable musicians held forth like this: "The ulterior motive behind the movement of collecting folk-songs, that has spread all over the world, is love of comfort. There is a desire: to become rejuvenated in this spring of freshness; a wish to revitalize the barren brain. This desire tries to hide an inner incompetence and to evade the struggle by comfortable and soul-killing devices."

This regrettable opinion is based on erroneous assumptions. These people must have a strange idea of the practice of composing. They seem to think the composer addicted to collecting folk-songs will sit down at his writing desk with the intention of composing a symphony; he racks and racks his brain but cannot think of a suitable melody; he takes up his collection of folk-songs, picks out one or two melodies and the composition of his symphony is done without further labour.

Well, it is not as simple as all that. It is a fatal error to attribute so much importance to the subject, the theme of a composition. We know that Shakespeare borrowed the stories of his plays from all sources. Does that prove that his brain was barren and he had to go to his neighbours begging for themes? Did he hide his incompetence? Molière's case is even worse. He not only borrowed the themes for his plays, but also part of the construction, and sometimes took over from his source expressions and whole lines unchanged.

We know that Handel adapted a work by Stradella in one of his oratorios. His adaptation is so masterly, so much surpassing the original in beauty, that we forget all about Stradella. Is there any sense in talking of plagiarism, of barrenness of brain, of incompetence in these cases?

In music it is the thematic material that corresponds to the story of a drama. And in music too, as in poetry and in painting, it does not signify what themes we use. It is the form into which we mould it that makes the essence of our work. This form reveals the knowledge, the creative power, the individuality of the artist.

The work of Bach is a summing up of the music of some hundred and odd years before him. His musical material is themes and motifs used by his predecessors. We can trace in Bach's music motifs, phrases which were also used by Frescobaldi and many others among Bach's predecessors. Is this plagiarism? By no means. For an artist it is not only right to have his roots in the art of some former times, it is a necessity.

Well, in our case it is peasant music which holds our roots.

The conception that attributes all that importance to the invention of a theme originated in the nineteenth century. It is a romantic conception which values originality above all.

From what has been said above, it must have become clear that it is no sign of "barrenness" or "incompetence" if a composer bases his music on folk-music instead of taking Brahms and Schumann as his models.

There exists another conception of modern music which seems exactly the opposite of the former one.

There are people who believe that nothing more is needed to bring about the full bloom in a nation's music than to steep oneself in folk-music and to transplant its motifs into established musical forms.

This opinion is founded on the same mistaken conception as the one discussed above. It stresses the all-importance of themes and forgets about the art of formation that alone can make something out of these themes. This process of moulding is the part of the composer's work which proves his creative talent.

And thus we may say: folk-music will become a source

of inspiration for a country's music only if the transplantation of its motifs is the work of a great creative talent. In the hands of incompetent composers neither folk-music nor any other musical material will ever attain significance. If a composer has no talent it will be of no use to him to base his music on folk-music or any other music. The result will in every case be nothing.

Folk-music will have an immense transforming influence on music in countries with little or no musical tradition. Most countries of southern and eastern Europe, including Hungary, are in this position.

May I, to conclude my thoughts, quote what Kodály once said in this context about the importance of folk-music.

"So little of written old Hungarian music has survived that the history of Hungarian music cannot be built up without a thorough knowledge of folk-music. It is known that folk language has many similarities with the ancient language of a people. In the same way folk-music must for us replace the remains of our old music. Thus, from a musical point of view, it means more to us than to those peoples that developed their own musical style centuries ago. Folk-music for these peoples became assimilated into their music, and a German musician will be able to find in Bach and Beethoven what we had to search for in our villages: the continuity of a national musical tradition."

2. ON COLLECTING FOLK SONGS IN TURKEY

(In 1937 Bartók accepted an invitation from the Turkish Government to lecture on Musical Folklore in Ankara and to assist it in organizing a collection of Turkish folk music.)

First of all, I must tell you which part of the country we wanted to explore. We went to Southern Anatolia, near the Syrian border, where the Yürüks have their winter camps. The Yürüks are a nomadic tribe who camp in the hilly parts of the south during winter and live high up in the Taurus mountain in summer. We assumed that a tribe that has still kept this ancestral form of life would very likely have preserved many of its old musical customs. That is why we cast our eyes on its land when setting out on our first journey.

The town Adana is the centre of this province and here we worked for the first two days rather successfully. The singers were sent to us from the surrounding villages. This arrangement did not conform with my ideas of collecting, according to which one has to go to the villages and live with the peasants. But I had to be careful after my illness of the previous week and could not risk living in a village in the first days.

On the third day we went to the small coastal town, Mersin, but there was very little we could take down here. Still, there were some compensations: this was a sub-tropical country and then, at the end of November, the weather was warm and lovely; we walked under banana trees in full bloom and covered with fruit, amidst blooming pepper trees, sugar canes, etc., dates around us and the temperature never falling to the point of frost.

At last on the fourth day we went to the part where the Yürüks lived, about 80 kilometres east of Adana. First we went to a biggish village, called Osmaniye. The people there and in the surrounding villages belong to a tribe, called "Ulas", which, for some reason or other, became permanently settled about seventy years ago.

We arrived at Osmaniye at 2 p.m. At four we entered the courtyard of a peasant house and I experienced deep joy because this was the real beginning of collecting peasant music as I had had it in my mind. The master of the house, Ali Bekir oglu Bekir, received us in a friendly way. When asked about his age he answered with some pride (through an interpreter) that in spite of his not having a tooth left he could still eat powerfully whatever he liked and that in spite of his seventy years he could run about in the mountains as quickly as a hare. We soon found out that he himself played an instrument, called "kemencse", which was a stringed instrument in the form of a "rehab". It is held in the old-fashioned way as a violoncello, though in size it is nearer to the violin and it is also tuned as a violin, only the a string is tuned in d.

There in the courtyard the old man started singing without much further ado. It was an old wartime epic he sang:

> "Kurt pasa cikli gozana
> Akil yetmez 'bu duzene . . ."

I could hardly believe my ears. Good Lord, this seemed to be the variation of an old Hungarian melody. I was overjoyed and made two records of this song sung by the old Bekir man.

Meanwhile the sun had set and we had to stop our work while our old friend and his people had their supper. This was Ramadan, a month of fast; for a whole month true believers were forbidden to eat during daytime. In the words of the Koran: the daily fast is at its end only when you cannot tell a white piece of string from a black one. The entire population is religious in this part of the world, even the black-coated officials of the villages are strict in keeping the fast. So the fast caused a little hitch in our plans.

The second melody the old Bekir gave us was again the

variation of a Hungarian melody. This was almost un-
canny, I thought. This song was sung in the interior of
the house, in a room which no woman was allowed to
enter. Sons of the old man and other people gathered
around us and gave us their songs, one after the other.
The whole evening was spent in work according to my
heart's desire. But it was not possible to get hold of a
woman singer. My companions might try as hard as they
could, they did not succeed in bringing one up.

The following day was to take us far to some nomadic
tribes, but an unexpected torrent of rain prevented our
going. The road was covered with a thick layer of mud
and the best car could not risk the journey. After a great
deal of dallying, we drove to a nearby village, Cardak. I
was firm that I would not start work if they did not send
me a woman singer.

Rather to my surprise a woman was found in a short
time, but we could not get out of her anything of value.
She sang two insignificant songs and that too in an un-
certain, haphazard fashion. I did not even take them
down. Then we tried our luck with a little boy and by
four o'clock I had taken down two or three melodies.
Then it seemed we had reached a complete deadlock. We
were rather sad and started packing our instruments with
the intention of going back to Osmaniye. Suddenly a
man addressed us: "It seems to me that the gentlemen
are not satisfied with what they have found here." "Indeed, no," was our reply, "we could hardly find anybody
able to sing." "Never mind," said the man (of whom we
later learned that he was a member of Parliament), "I
know my people well enough and shall send you crowds
of singers. It will be quite a job for you to hear them
all."

He was as good as his word. He called together a big

gathering at the school hall, invited two musicians from a neighbouring village, and the people began dancing. And what a dance this was! The music was strange, almost frightening. One of the musicians played an instrument, called "zurna", which was a kind of oboe of very sharp tones; the other had a big drum, called "davul", slung over his shoulder. He beat his drum, using a wooden stick, with a diabolical fierceness, so that I expected that either his drum or my ear drums would split at any moment. Even the flame of our oil lamp, flickering so peacefully, leapt high at every beat! And the dance! Four men performed it, one as a "solo dancer", the other three linked together, accompanying him with a few scanty movements only. At intervals the musicians, too, entered the dance with accompanying steps and movements. All of a sudden the music came to an end, the dancing stopped and a song broke forth. One of the three accompanying men had started singing, sunk in himself with an expression of devotion that I cannot describe in words. He started the song on the highest note of his high tenor voice and moved slowly downwards, as the song neared its end, to more human spheres.

I really had reason to feel ashamed of the shabbiness and inadequacy of my recording apparatus. But the best apparatus would still have been less than good enough to do justice to this incomparable scene we witnessed. It should have been filmed by a very clever artist. There was one factor only that acted as a damper on the fantastic beauty of the scene, and that was the complete absence of old national costumes. All the people wore ordinary shabby suits as worn by Western factory workers. I really could not tell how it was possible that these hideous suits had found their way to the nomadic tribes of the Yürüks and their descendants, whilst in Transylvania and in the Balkans we still could find the most picturesque national costumes.

The following day our plans were upset by heavy rain. After long discussions and a short but adventurous motor drive, we arrived at the village Toprakale and hired a cart which took us on roads (that were not even too unmanageable) to a tent village in which a tribe lived in completely unchanged nomadic conditions. We arrived at noon, but could soon perceive that this was no field for our work. The men were away; the women, of course, were at home, but under no conditions would they open their mouths and sing us songs without their husbands' permitting them to do so.

On we went then to the next camp of nomadic tribes. Our cart drove across rivers (big and small), the road grew stonier and ceased altogether, and our cart just went on and on rattling over rocky hillsides. This manner of travelling was not very pleasant. It might have been all right without the care of our instruments. But we had to keep the phonographs and the records firmly on our laps. At last we had enough of that business; we walked on, on foot, carrying our fragile treasures on our backs and in our hands. At sunset we at last reached the winter camp of a tribe, called Tecirli. They are also a nomadic tribe, but live in clay huts and not in tents for the winter. Our guide took us to the "house" of a man who seemed rather influential among the families of the tribe, and whom he knew well. This man received us most amiably. A well-mannered and tactful man, he did not ask questions about the purpose of our visit or about the funny apparatus we carried with us. He at once ordered a sheep to be killed for our meal, but we said a hen would be sufficient. He invited us to enter his house and we entered a dwelling completely dark and with no windows. There were mattresses in rows along the walls and a fireplace in the middle of the room. Following the local customs, we took off our shoes and were seated in the Turkish way on the mattresses, whilst our host laid a fire. There was no chimney, no window. In a few seconds the room was filled with the most suffocating smoke. If on the previous night our ear drums had had to withstand a heavy assault, it was now the turn of our eyes! There was nothing to complain about. Fortunately, it did not take long before the fire burnt with high flames and the smoke found its way out through gaps in the scantily-built walls.

Slowly the room got filled with people from the neighbourhood and we talked and talked very amicably. This went on till seven, and apparently our guide had not even mentioned yet what had brought us here. I was sitting on coals. At seven I heard our guide saying words like "turku", "turk halk musiki", etc. At last I could hear that folk songs were mentioned and hoped the ice would soon be broken. And indeed, without shyness and hesitation a fifteen-year-old boy sang the first song, and it was again a melody that sounded Hungarian to me. I quickly prepared my instruments on the mattresses spread out on the floor and took down the song in writing by the light of the wood fire. Well, I thought, now let us begin with the recording. But this did not prove as easy as all that. My good singer was frightened he might lose his voice by singing into a machine obviously driven by a devil; this instrument, he thought, might not only take down his voice, but take it away altogether. It took me long to dispel his fright. Then we worked incessantly, undisturbed till midnight. I thought the time had then come to ask a few delicate questions, especially regarding women. Whether women sing other songs than men. "Oh, no, by no means", was the short but decided answer. Well,

I went on, but surely they knew the same songs and it would be so nice for us to hear these songs sung by women. After some embarrassment they informed us that women never sang in the presence of men. Not even a husband had the right to ask his wife for a song. I had to resign myself to this fact, since naturally I could not claim rights greater than those of a husband, and gave up all hope with a sad heart. What a pity! And to know that there in the house were the wives—more than one—of our host! Back in Ankara I told my employers that something had to be done about this question. Either they should send out women on journeys of collection or the male collectors should be accompanied by their wives, who could then deal with the women. It is an impossible situation to have to record lullabies in croaking men's voices when it was obvious that men never lulled their babies to sleep with or without songs!

This night with the nomadic tribes at Tecirli was the conclusion of my journey. It had been my intention so to arrange my journey in every detail that I could present my Turkish employers with a model of collecting technique which they could follow up in future cases. I must own that what I achieved did not come up to my standard of perfection. At the very outset I had the bad luck to be unwell and unable to go out to the villages for three days. Then there was the great shortcoming that we were unable to obtain all relevant information regarding the songs we had collected (when, where, by whom were the songs sung, how had they been handed down, etc.). And the information we had obtained was not always correct. The data we had put down were sometimes contradictory. This was partly due to the shortness of time at our disposal. If we had been more persistent in pursuing these data we could have spent less time on the collection of melodies. Then, of course, I was greatly handicapped in my work by not being able to talk to people myself but only through an interpreter. I was unable to find out whether two or more people ever sang together, and if so on what occasions. The fact is that I could never get people to sing together, not even people who lived in the same village. All my trials resulted in a complete failure, which would indicate that singing in chorus was unknown among people in this part of the world. But even that statement should be accepted with caution. It is almost unthinkable that Turkish people should never sing together, never form a chorus (if only in one voice). Then the greatest shortcoming, that we were unable to hear women singing. But I have spoken about that already. And finally, the texts could not always be taken down completely and were mostly preserved only by the phonograph records.

In spite of all these shortcomings, I think the collection we made is interesting and valuable, and contains some scientifically useful discoveries. The most important of these is a melody of a definite character recurring everywhere in the area (of about 80 kilometres diameter) where we had worked. About twenty out of the ninety melodies we collected belong to this recurring type. The character of these melodies shows striking similarities with the downward moving construction of old Hungarian melodies. The melody starts on the highest note and moves downward, reaching the lowest note somewhere near the end of the song, the difference being that the Hungarian songs start on the octave whilst the Turkish songs on the tenth note (octave —2). The closing note is the lowest in the Turkish songs, whilst in Hungarian songs the melody frequently moves one or two notes below that. The Turkish melodies are richer in decorative motifs, which sometimes differ from those found in Hungarian melodies. They are not based on a pentatonic scale, but written in a "Dorian" mode. It may be though that the origin of both is the pentatonic scale. Very important is a negative conclusion: the complete absence of Arabic influence, unless found in a few decorative phrases.

The remaining seventy melodies cannot easily be classed in groups. In some of them I found a type of rhythm of changing punctuation known to me from my Hungarian material. I do not know whether these changes are due to adaptations to texts and more material would be needed to prove this.